THE BLUE-EYED IROQUOIS

THE BLUE-EYED IROQUOIS

By Edith A. Hough

1984

NORTH COUNTRY BOOKS

18 Irving Place

Utica, NY 13501

First Paperback Printing 1984
NORTH COUNTRY BOOKS

ISBN 978-0-932052-30-8

Printed in the United States of America
Maple-Vail Book Manufacturing Group

DEDICATION

This book is dedicated to the memory of my mother, Effie Caughey Hough, who was born near Wellington, Ontario; and to my father, William Henry Hough, who was born at Lower Ireland, Megantic County, Quebec. As young people, they came to the United States, finally settling in Syracuse, New York where they met and were married.

FOREWORD

About the middle of the seventeenth century, Pierre Esprit Radisson came from France, with his family, to settle in Three Rivers, Quebec, near Montreal, in Canada.

At this time, the powerful federation of Iroquois Indians lived in what is now central New York State. They held absolute control of the fur trading from the present Canadian border through most of what is now the eastern United States. And they were mortal enemies of the Canadian Indians against whom they made frequent raids.

The Iroquois federation consisted of five (later six) "nations" or tribes. Of these, the Mohawks were the fiercest warriors.

It was on one of the raiding forays of these Mohawks that they captured young Radisson (then only 16) and carried him back to their home in what is now central New York State. There he was adopted by a Mohawk chief. And he was destined to become one of the co-founders of the Hudson Bay Fur Trading Company and be known as "King of the Fur Traders."

Historians believe Radisson was the first white person to see the country east of the present city of Syracuse, New York, and to gaze at Niagara Falls.

The following tale is the story of his capture and torture by the Mohawks and his attempts to escape and return to his home at Three Rivers, Quebec.

TABLE OF CONTENTS

Page

CHAPTER I

Pierre Radisson stepped from the darkened interior of his log cabin home, and out into the magic brightness of a spring day. He threw back his head, closed his blue eyes, and stood with the sun shining full on his young face and fair hair. The sun's warmth seemed to soak into his skin and spread all through his body. How good it felt!

As he stood there, he was dimly aware that inside the cabin, his sister, Margaret, and his mother were chatting together as they went about the work of washing the dinner dishes. And he knew his father was enjoying his after-dinner pipe as he sat by the fireplace.

But Pierre's thoughts were not on his family just now. His delight was in the realization that, at last, spring had actually come. A soft breeze blew across his face, and he drew such a deep breath that it almost made him dizzy. Even his fingers and toes tingled. Suddenly, he opened his eyes and looked at the familiar view of the neighbors' log cabin homes, and beyond them, to the top of the stockade which surrounded this little village of Three Rivers. How many times he had stared at the same scene all through the long winter months! And now that spring had come, how he longed to stretch his legs outside that stockade, and to explore the unknown land beyond.

But he could hear his father's voice, as plainly as if he stood beside him, saying,

"Remember, Pierre, you must never go outside the stockade. Those Iroquois Indians from south of the river are not to be trusted. They are not like our neighbors, the friendly Algonquin Indians. Those Iroquois would kill you if they saw you alone. Stay inside the stockade, where you are safe!"

How tiresome that was. Pierre thought to himself as he kicked at a clod of earth. If only he could go outside, even

11

for just a little way — just far enough to see what the country was like! He frowned to himself. Surely there could be no harm in going to the stockade gate and looking out. Slowly, he wandered down St. Louis Street. Several friends and neighbors were outside their log cabin houses — some working in their gardens — and they called greetings to him. A few children paused long enough in their playing to say "hello." He was pleased at all these signs of friendliness and he answered pleasantly enough, as was his custom. But he felt distracted today and he did not linger to talk with any of them.

As he reached the end of St. Louis Street, he came to the southeast gate of the protecting walls of the stockade. Pierre felt a glow of pride as he raised his eyes to the pointed tips of those bark-free upright logs fastened so tightly together. Monsieur LeFord and Monsieur Dandonneau had done a fine piece of work in directing the building of this protecting wall. How could the settlement ever have warded off the attacking Indians these past months without them? It was a fine fortress, strong, and well-built.

From where he stood by the gateway, he gazed back at the thirty buildings of the settlement. On his left were the home of the Jesuits, and the Chapel of the Savages. Here he had seen Christian Indians bringing choice pieces of deer meat to leave at the altar as sacrifices when they came to give thanks for a successful hunt. Past the chapel he could see one corner of the Governor's home, and beyond that, part of the house where the soldiers were quartered. In the far corner of the stockade wall toward the northeast, rose the watch tower. How safe it made Pierre feel! But he turned and gazed through the gateway of the stockade.

"I wish I could go outside", he thought again. "Wouldn't it be exciting to explore this new land? Surely, I can step through the gate! That would not be dangerous."

Just outside, a sentry was pacing up and down.

"Good afternoon, Pierre", he called.

Pierre waved his hand and smiled in friendly greeting.

"Good afternoon, Monsieur Pepin." Then, in a joking voice, "Any Indians to-day?"

Monsieur Pepin patted his musket as he transferred it to his other shoulder.

"You'd have heard a shot from this if there were."

Pierre became sober.

"Yes, I know", he said.

Monsieur Pepin rested the butt of his musket on the ground.

"You know, Pierre, these Iroquois Indians are a terrible lot. Awful fighters. But then, even if you did just come over from France last year, I guess you've seen and heard enough about their murdering ways to know all you want to about them."

Pierre nodded, absently. For a few moments, neither one spoke. Then Pierre, rested his gaze on the sparkling expanse of the broad St. Lawrence River. A dreamy expression crossed his attractive features.

"It is a beautiful river, isn't it, Monsieur Pepin? I wonder how much further it goes? I wonder what the lands beyond are like."

Monsieur Pepin was emphatic in his answer.

"You'd better not try to find out, Pierre." He pointed to the south, across the river. "Away off beyond there, is where those Iroquois Indians come from. You know, as well as I, how many of our people have been killed by these savages right here. What chance would anyone have outside where he wasn't protected?"

Pierre nodded. He knew the Iroquois had harrassed them all winter. He knew that safety demanded that the white people stay inside the stockade walls; and yet, inwardly, Pierre rebelled. He was so weary of all this waiting. Had he and his family come such a great distance to this new country only to spend all their time inside a fortress? For the hundredth time, Pierre rebelled at his fate.

Just then, someone in the gateway called a "good afternoon", and Pierre and Monsieur Pepin turned to see the short, fat figure of Antoine Desrosiers. As the two men drifted into a conversation which did not especially interest him, Pierre wandered a little away from them along the outside wall of the stockade, kicking at the tall grass as he went.

The bright sunlight made him squint. Now that it was warm enough to plant corn, perhaps those Iroquois Indians would no longer want to be on the warpath, but would go back home. Then, it would be safe to go out along the river bank and even into the woods; safe to investigate the neighboring countryside.

Again his eyes sought the distant blue across the great river. As he gazed at the unbroken stretches of forest, its bright new leaves in contrast with the occasional darker accents of evergreen, his imagination was stirred. What lay beyond? As he wondered, a great resolution gripped him. Some day he would explore this vast new country. With his own eyes, he, Pierre Radisson would see land which no white man had ever beheld! Somehow, sometime, he would do it. He jammed his hands into the pockets of his brown homespun trousers and kicked the toe of one shoe into the soft earth.

But, as his resolution took shape, little did Pierre realize how quickly it was to turn into actuality, nor to what adventures and suffering it would lead.

CHAPTER II

As Pierre was thinking over his new resolution, he was concentrating so hard that he did not notice two of his friends coming toward him through the stockade gate. Nor did he hear them greet Monsieur Desrosieres and Monsieur Pepin; and he was startled when they called him by name. He turned, quickly.

"Oh, hello, Francois! Hello, Jean!" he answered.

The two boys linked arms with Pierre and pulled him back inside the stockade gate.

"Come on over here where that guard can't hear us," whispered Jean.

"Yes," Francois said in a quiet voice, "we've been looking all over for you." Then, glancing about to see that there was no one else nearby, he added, "Want to go outside hunting to-morrow?"

Pierre's heart leaped. Of course he did! Then, suddenly, the light died out of his eyes, for once again he remembered his father's often repeated warning. "Never go outside the stockade alone, Pierre, for those Indians are as cunning as foxes. They rise up from nowhere, and, almost before you realize they are anywhere nearby, they might capture or kill you!"

Seeing Pierre's hesitation, Jean shrugged his shoulders and half turned away.

"Of course, if you're afraid . . . .," he taunted.

Pierre grasped him by the arm and whirled him around.

"Who says I'm afraid? I'm sixteen; and I can shoot as well as you, even if you are a little older."

Francois and Jean laughed at his flushed face and angry eyes.

"Then you'll come?" asked Francois.

"Good! Meet us behind the Chapel just before sun-up. Don't tell anyone!"

15

Pierre promised, and he whistled happily to himself as he hurried home.

At the back door, his father was chopping wood, and Pierre wondered if his face showed a guilty expression, but when his father merely nodded absently to him, Pierre was relieved. He must not let his family suspect the excitement and joy that was making his heart pound. Hoping not to betray himself, he picked up his own hatchet from the bench at the doorway and silently helped his father for a little while. Then, just as quietly and, he hoped, casually, he entered the back door of his log-cabin home.

Pierre's sister, Margaret, was setting the table, and his mother was taking bread from the oven which was built into one side of the fireplace. As she set it out to cool, she spoke to Pierre. "If you go out again, don't be gone long, dear, for supper will soon be ready."

Pierre tried to sound natural. "I'll be right around here, Mother." And he walked slowly past her, skirted the table and stood leaning against the farther wall. Seeing that his mother and Margaret were paying him no special attention, he set one foot on the lowest rung of the loft ladder and very quietly climbed through the hole in the ceiling to the second floor where they all slept.

Softly drawing back the curtain which marked off his corner of the loft, he crawled stealthily under the bed and pulled out his musket and powder horn. Then he listened, fearful that his mother might call out to ask what he was doing. But only the reassuring clatter of the supper preparations floated up through the opening in the floor.

Having examined his musket to see that it was clean, and finding his powder horn filled, he slid them back under his bed and crept back down the ladder just as Margaret was calling their father to supper.

All during the meal Pierre was fearful that some of his family might notice his excitement. To cover it, he ate slowly, and pretended to pay rapt attention to whatever was

16

discussed at the table. Once, he thought his father looked questioningly in his direction; but just then his mother asked if he would have more cornmeal mush, and Pierre breathed more easily.

Supper over, Margaret washed the dishes, while Pierre lay on the bearskin rug before the dying embers of the fire and listened to his father telling his mother of one of their neighbor's hunting trips. Pierre wanted to say, "I'm going, too, Father! In the morning, I am going, too!" But he kept his own council, and waited impatiently for bedtime to come. At last it grew dark, and his mother asked Margaret to light a candle. Soon, his father finished his story, and having smoked his pipe for a little while, he yawned, stretched, and said,

"Well, I guess it is time to go to bed. Come, Pierre light a candle, and off to bed with you."

Pierre did as he was told and climbed to his loft bedroom. He did not undress before crawling under the homemade quilts; nor did he try to go to sleep. He lay quietly listening to his mother and Margaret fussing down below. He heard his father come up the ladder and listened to hear his boots dropped on the floor. Then, after a time, Margaret came up; and, at last, his mother.

It seemed hours before Pierre could be sure they were all asleep. Then, as quietly as he could, he crawled out from under the covers, and kneeling down drew out his musket and powder horn from under the bed. He would hide them outside the cabin, and then, if his family heard him when morning came, he could simply pretend he was getting up early.

It was so dark in the cabin that Pierre could scarcely find his way, but he must make no sound. Above all, he must not stumble or fall. With powder horn slung over his shoulder and his musket under one arm, he inched his way cautiously across the floor. Then he stopped and listened. Were they all fast asleep? The sound of deep breathing reassured him.

17

He must be near the opening for the ladder. Dropping softly on all fours, he felt around the floor with his free hand. Ah! There was the top of the ladder!

When he was half way down, Pierre felt that he dared to breathe naturally. It was easy, then, to feel his way safely around the familiar table, past the fireplace, and over to the cabin door. With his hands on the latch, he listened once more. All was still. The silence was so great it seemed to prickle in his ears.

Satisfied, Pierre opened the door, crept over to some bushes, and hid his musket and powder horn among them. Then, just as quietly as he had gone out, he reentered the cabin and crept up the ladder and into bed. For a long time he lay there, his heart pounding with suppressed excitement. At last he slept fitfully, and, rousing suddenly, toward morning, he picked up his boots and once more crept quietly downstairs.

Pierre shivered as he rummaged for some breakfast. Stuffing a few pieces of bread and some cold meat into his pockets, he tiptoed to the door and stepped outside. As he closed the door quietly behind him, little did he realize how very long it would be before he would again step through that cabin doorway.

Picking up his musket and powder horn, he hurried down the street. The sky in the east was just beginning to show faint streaks of light. He must hurry! As he approached the gateway, he could see two forms huddled there.

"Hello!" they whispered. Then, with no more conversation the three boys slid softly through the southeast gateway.

The sentry was not more than ten feet away, but by flattening themselves against the wall, the boys successfully worked their way around the corner of the stockade. In the semidarkness, the mill, the protecting redoubt, and the cannon which stood not far from the fortress loomed up like sinister and accusing shadows.

18

As they walked through the long grass, Pierre's conscience troubled him. In the cold dawn, some of his first excitement began to wear away. He shivered a little. Perhaps he should have said something to his family about going hunting. But, after all, was he not almost a man? And was it not time he was making some of his own decisions? Besides, his father had said never go alone; and was he not with two other boys? Surely, three of them could keep a sharp watch for any hostile Indians!

Pierre noticed how happy his two companions were; and he too, felt his spirits rising. This was more like it! He gazed out over the great river. How cool and inviting it looked with the sun just rising over the distant hills! Some day he would cross that river; and he would explore the virgin forest, seeing what lay beyond. He would push westward, ... on and on. No one knew how far the land extended, but some day, he felt sure, he, Pierre Esprit Radisson, would find out. Suddenly, he felt sure this was to be his purpose in life, — exploring, and perhaps even trading with the Indians.

Just then, Francois grasped his arm and motioned for him to be still, for someone was coming toward the fortress. The boys hid behind some bushes and waited, breathlessly. Every second seemed an hour. Then, to their relief, they saw it was a Frenchman, and they stepped out to greet him.

"Hello," they said.

For an answer, he shook his head at them.

"Lads," he questioned, "I do hope you are going no further?"

The boys hesitated.

"Well," faltered Pierre, "we were just going to do a little hunting."

Again the man shook his head.

"Don't be foolish, lads. Indians are hiding all round here. They are not like our neighbors, the friendly Hurons and Algonquins. These are the fierce Iroquois from far south of

the river. They are very warlike and cruel. Why, just now,
I've been talking with a man who pastures cattle near here.
And he says you never can tell where they are. One minute,
there is nothing to be seen but the grass and the trees. Then,
before you can wink your eye, a hundred heads appear in the
long grass. And you know what happens then!"

He looked sharply at them as he added, "You'd best go
back where it is safe!"

But his words only made the boys more stubborn.

"We're tired of staying in the fortress," Francois replied.
"Anyway," he added, "I guess three of us can watch out for
Indians."

"Of course we can!" echoed Pierre, as he raised his head
and straightened his shoulders.

The man pleaded with them, but, when he saw they could
not be persuaded, he left with a final warning,

"Then if you must go, keep to the rivers edge. It will be
easier to watch from there. And don't go into the woods, or
back toward the mountains; for that's where those Indians
hide. Remember, keep to the river bank!"

After he was gone, the boys counselled together.

"Two of us could stay by the river bank," said Pierre.
"and the other one could go into the edge of the woods to
watch. Then, those Indians could not sneak up on us!"

"Sure!" the others agreed. "That way we will be safe. You
go into the edge of the woods, Pierre, and we'll stay by the
river bank. How will you let us know if you see anything?"

"I could whistle!" answered Pierre.

The boys nodded. "Keep watch of us, too, Pierre. Don't
get out of sight."

"I won't," he promised.

Walking back from the river bank, Pierre crept quietly
along among the trees. His ears were alert for any sound and
his quickly darting eyes were on the lookout for any suspicious
movement of leaves or shadows. Frequently he turned around
to be sure he could still see the boys.

All was quiet in the forest. Only the snapping of an occasional dry twig under his feet broke the silence. Pierre crept ahead, slowly and cautiously. There seemed to be nothing to fear.

Then, suddenly, the sharp crack of a musket shot rang out from not far off. Frightened, Pierre dropped to the ground and flattened himself as best he could against the trunk of a large tree. He waited, his heart pounding in terror. Then he heard the boy's voices. "We've got a duck, Pierre!"

Pierre breathed his relief and dared to raise himself to a standing position. He laughed as he walked between the trees to where Jean and Francois could see him.

"Good for you!" he called. "I thought it was an Indian taking a shot at me."

Jean pointed to Francois who was wadding and reloading his musket from his powder horn. "There's your Indian," he smiled.

Pierre grinned. "That's the kind I like." he answered. and stepped back among the trees.

From time to time he heard the boys shooting, and each time, he carefully made certain it was they, and not any hostile Indians. At last, he himself had an opportunity at a shot, and his excitement and joy at getting a squirrel made him forget his fears and the gnawing of his conscience over having come on this hunting trip without letting his people know.

For several hours they hunted, and, at last growing weary, Pierre crept back to the river bank and met his friends. All of them threw themselves down full length on the grass in the warm sunshine.

"This is more like it!" Pierre sighed as he stretched and gazed up into the bright blue sky. "I was so tired of looking at nothing but the inside of that fortress.' '

He raised himself on one elbow.

"Let's see how much we got altogether."

Jean began to count. "Five ducks, three geese, two squirrels, . . ."

Pierre interrupted.

"I almost got a fox!"

Jean and Francois laughed. "I'll bet you did!"

"But I did, too." protested Pierre. "When I pulled the trigger, the flint didn't spark; so he got away!"

Jean went on with his counting.

"And two beaver. I think that is about enough."

Pierre was surprised. Quickly, he raised himself to a sitting position.

"Enough!" he exclaimed. "Don't tell me you are going to stop now! Why, we've hardly started yet!"

"I know," replied Jean, "but we've all the meat our families can eat before it would spoil."

Francois glanced toward the dense woods. "I think we should go back, Pierre. After all, just because we've seen no Indians doesn't mean they aren't somewhere nearby. We've had fun. Let's go home now and come back another day."

But Pierre shrugged his shoulders.

"You make me tired!" he exclaimed. "We come out to hunt, and what happens? Almost as soon as we get started, you two want to go back home! Let's get a fox before we quit. We're all right! You see how we watched and watched for Indians, and there were none!"

"But, Pierre, ..."

"Well, you didn't see any Indians, did you?"

"No, but that's just it. You don't see them until it's too late."

By this time, Pierre was walking back and forth, and his blue eyes flashed as he said,

"Well, you go home if you like! But I'm going to stay, Indians or no Indians. I guess I can take care of myself. And if you're both such old women, you can go back without me!"

22

Jean and Francois tried to argue with Pierre, but it was of no use. Pierre was cocky by this time.

"Just wait till I come back with a deer and perhaps even a bear!" he taunted. "Then, I guess you'll be sorry you didn't come." And he picked up his musket and walked into the woods.

"We just hope you will not be the sorry one!" Jean and Francois called after him.

CHAPTER III

Pierre felt much freer without the two boys, for now, he could go on as he pleased. Eagerly, he looked about him for he had never been this far way from the stockade before. But, keen as he was to explore, he knew he must be very cautious. So, hiding behind trees, listening carefully, and ever on the lookout, Pierre crept on, finding plenty to shoot at. At last he had ten ducks, three geese, and a crane. Suddenly he noticed that the sun was beginning to get lower in the sky, so he decided he had better turn toward home.

Since he had too much game to carry, he began to look around for some place to hide part of it. There was a hollow tree! Tomorrow, he could bring his father and some friends to get the rest. How proud his family would be when they saw all the fresh meat he had shot! Perhaps, when they knew how well he could take care of himself, they would let him go hunting again. Then he would not have to steal away. How he would laugh at Jean and Francois for going back so soon! With part of the game hidden, and the rest slung over his shoulder, he turned back toward home.

By the time he was within a short distance of where he had left his companions, Pierre suddenly realized how tired he was. Maybe he should sit down and rest for a few minutes. Surely he was safe, so close to the fortress that he could practically make himself heard if he shouted! And, besides, perhaps the boys had waited for him, after all.

As he sat down, he glanced about, but saw no one. Then, suddenly he heard a soft, almost imperceptible sound; and, Raising himself cautiously and glancing in all directions, he walked off about thirty paces to investigate. All he saw were some wild ducks swimming in a little brook nearby. Surely there could be no one else about if the ducks had not taken fright; and he might as well bag a few to add to his collection. Raising his musket, he took careful aim. But

24

Pierre never shot any of these ducks, for, just then, something in the tall grass by the edge of the stream caught his eye. Was that a hand? Frozen with horror, Pierre remained crouched in shooting position. Then, as he realized that this was a hand, and a white person's hand, he inched cautiously forward, his musket ever ready. Fear tensed his muscles, and his fast beating heart nearly choked him. As he edged around a small bush, he stopped, his eyes widening in sudden horror. For there partly hidden in the long grass, lay the lifeless bodies of Jean and Francois, blood still streaming from hatchet blows on their hands and faces, and matting their curly brown hair.

Pierre felt sick and faint at the sight. Utter panic seized him. Why had they come hunting? Why had he not obeyed his father? His father! And his mother! Would he ever see them again? If only he had stayed home!

But suddenly, Pierre knew this was no time to consider his feelings. He realized there was nothing he could possibly do for his friends, and, for his own safety, he must get to the river bank as quickly as possible! That was his only hope! Even now, Indians might be hidden, watching his every move, and ready to pounce on him without warning. Bending forward, the better to hide in the long grass, he crept cautiously, but hurriedly, forward. He was almost at the river!

And then, between him and the river half a hundred Indian heads rose silently from the grass! What should he do? He could not go through them, and, if he turned back into the woods, how did he know how many other Indians might be there? If only he could creep on all fours through the tall grass, he might not be noticed by them! Then, once at the river someone from the fortress might see him; or the Indians might be afraid of being too conspicuous there, and they might not try to follow him so close to the settlement. How he hoped they had not yet seen him!

But just then, an arrow twanged over his head, scarcely missing him. So, he shot back. If he could not escape, at least he would fight! But almost before he could load his musket again, the Indians were closing in on him, . . . throwing him to the ground, and holding him tightly. More and more Indians ran up, shouting and yelling wildly in their joy over his capture. Yet, even then, Pierre dared to hope that the sentry at the stockade might hear them and send some men to rescue him.

But this was not to be. And, in spite of his struggles, the Indians bound him, then half dragged and half carried him to the river's edge where they threw him into the bottom of a canoe and paddled swiftly away.

Pierre tried to raise his head, but one of the young Indians pushed it down, merely laughing at his struggles. Even if he could not see them all, Pierre knew this was no small band of Indians, for he could hear the soft gurgle of many paddles; and his heart sank at the realization. And so, wretched and uncomfortable, he lay wondering what his fate was to be. Would they kill him, too, as they had Jean and Francois? If so, he prayed they might do it quickly, for he had heard enough of Indian tortures not to know what might lie in store for him. He studied the young Indian who had pushed him into the bottom of the canoe. His hair, shaven on each side, except for one long lock, and cut in crested form on top of his head, gave proof that these belonged to the Mohawk tribe of the Iroquois Indians. Pierre had heard great tales of these Indians. He knew they were fierce fighters, that they, with the Oneidas, the Onondagas, the Senecas and the Cayugas were joined in a league, and that all these tribes were called by the one name of Iroquois. So great was their strength, through uniting, that they controlled vast territories to the south of the St. Lawrence River.

Pierre judged they must have traveled some four or five miles from Three Rivers when the Indians stopped and, beaching their canoes, they laughed and chattered jubilantly as they dragged him into the woods.

26

Pierre hated the odor of these hundred or so dirty savages as some of them threw him to the ground and crowded about him. Their semi-naked and sweaty bodies, their paint-daubed faces, and the strong odor of bear's grease rubbed into their crested-cut hair, made him feel sick! If only he could see a white man's face! Loud with glee, they yanked and tore at his clothing, seeming to enjoy themselves more if they could twist his arms and legs while they were stripping him naked. Then, two Indians, one young and one older brave, stepped up, laughing and poking their fingers into his soft, white flesh as they tied a rope about his waist. Next, they jerked him to his feet by each end of the rope, and chattered together in amusement at his shivering form.

In spite of his misery, Pierre noticed with surprise these evidences of humor in the Indians. He had known them only as soberfaced and impassive traders, or hard and cruel warriors.

Meanwhile, the Indians were preparing to camp for the night. Pierre watched while some gathered wood, others unpacked baskets of cornmeal and bear's grease. Some sat by the river and smeared this grease all over their hair; others produced chunks of raw meat which looked as if it had been carried for some time. Several speared fish; and a few were kindling fires by rubbing two sticks together. To do this, they hollowed out a small piece of very old, dry wood, dropped in some powdered bark and powdered-dried grass, and, holding a small pointed stick upright between their palms, they revolved the stick rapidly. After some time, a few sparks began to fly. Indians crouching near the fire makers blew gently at the sparks, and soon the powdered tinder burst into flame. As the flames grew brighter, Pierre's fears increased. Were they going to torture him by fire?

He gritted his teeth and clenched his fists. How he hated them! Why should they do this to him? What had he ever done to deserve this? And then, once again his conscience rose to bother him; for was not this the very thing his father

27

had warned him against? How he wished he had never gone hunting!

Just then, some Indian scouts ran up. Pierre wished he could speak the Mohawk language so he could know what they were saying. They were jabbering excitedly and pointing back in the direction of Three Rivers. Had his people discovered these Indians, and were they coming after him?

While some of the younger Indians hurried to throw water and dirt on their fires, the others pulled all the canoes into the shelter of overhanging bushes along the shore, the older braves grasped Pierre and forced him to hide in the bushes. One especially dirty savage drew Pierre into a vise-like grip and pressed his hand against his mouth to prevent his making a sound. Through the bushes Pierre could see all the other Indians scurrying to crawl into the scrub growth, or stand behind the larger tree trunks.

Pierre's hopes rose. Perhaps the French had missed him and were coming, after all. His heart beat quickly as he strained his ears for any slight sounds. For a long time they waited and waited while Pierre's hopes soared, faded, and then died. At last the Indians came out from their hiding places, rekindled their fires, and once more set about getting their suppers.

Pierre felt sick at heart. Watching the Indians at their cooking, he remembered how good the French food was; and how clean and warm was his mother's kitchen back home. She was probably worrying about him right now, as she cooked supper for the rest of the family. He swallowed hard, and then forced himself to watch the Indians again.

How dirty they looked! Several were coming toward him — one had a slight limp and a wound down one side of his face which gave him an ugly leer. Another had such well-developed muscles that they rippled as he walked; and a third carried Pierre's clothing. What were they going to do to him?

First, they gave him back his clothes. Then, the one with the ugly leer held him and laughed with childish jubilation while the others combed his hair and smeared it with smelly bear's grease. It had a sickening odor but Pierre dared not let them know how he hated what they were doing. So he tried to smile; but he feared it was a weak effort. Next, they put red paint all over his face, and, continuing their laughing and jabbering, they brought him some of their food. He had watched them place strips of raw meat on some stones heated near the fire, and after leaving it for ten or fifteen minutes, he had been almost sick at seeing them take it in both hands and chew ravenously while the blood ran down on each side of their mouths.

As they approached him, the smell of the half-spoiled meat cooked in yellow meal made Pierre nauseated; but he dared not let them know how he felt. What unknown torture might lie in store for him if he refused to eat? So, shutting his eyes, he chewed and swallowed.

More and more Indians were clustering around him now and viewing him as if he were some great curiosity. One very powerfully-built young Indian who was taller than the rest strode arrogantly up to Pierre and slapped his face.

Pierre's anger rose. Doubling up his fists he struck out at the young brave. But before they could come to blows, two older warriors pulled him away while the arrogant one laughed. But Pierre noticed that the rest did not join with him, and he saw two young Indians looking him over as if to measure his strength against that of his larger opponent. Did they not like this arrogant one, or did they have a sense of fair play after all?

When at last nightfall came, the Indians stripped him once more, made sure the rope around his waist was secure; and then they forced him to lie between two older warriors, each of whom held one end of the rope. Even if Pierre had dared to think of trying to escape before, he knew now, that it was hopeless.

"But surely," he thought to himself, "some chance will come. I must be alert and ready to snatch at it. Since they have not killed me yet, perhaps I did the right thing in trying to fight that young Indian. If they stay camped here for a while, they may not keep me tied up all the time, and perhaps I can steal away."

But for the present, he must make the best of his fate and try to sleep. If he could rest, he might feel stronger for whatever ordeals were awaiting him. But the torture of myriads of mosquitoes constantly attacking the whole of his naked body, and his ever-present thoughts of home kept him from closing his eyes all night long. Only the Indians appeared to be resting under the protection of their blankets. But if Pierre so much as stirred to brush off some of the mosquitoes, his guards seemed to sense it, and they pulled the rope more tightly around him. It cut into his flesh. It was hard to say which was worse — the rope, or the itching mosquito bites. Since he dared not move to brush off the mosquitoes, he tried blowing his breath hard across his chest. But it seemed to have no effect upon the singing, torturing mosquitoes. It was a long night for Pierre.

CHAPTER IV

The next morning Pierre decided the Indians must be taking him back to their homes, for, having bound him, and tied him to the bar in a canoe, they travelled all day, further and further away from his home at Three Rivers. He could only guess at how many miles they covered; but he knew from the position of the sun that they were going west, and a little south.

Late in the afternoon, they came to some islands where there was room for all the party of about two hundred and fifty to camp. Apparently thinking they would be safe, they settled down to several days of hunting. Again, Pierre thought of trying to steal off; he could find his way by following the river. But the Indians kept too close a watch, and he knew he dared not attempt it. To be caught would mean sure torture and death.

And, by now, Pierre had decided that he very much wanted to live. Bound as he had been, and with no one to talk to, and no chance to do anything but think, he had made up his mind that, no matter to what tortures he might be subjected, he would show the spirit of a true Frenchman. He would prove to these savages that he was a man; he would accept his lot, no matter what. Then, if they spared his life, he would learn all he could about them — how they lived, and how they fought; and if he could escape back home, he would return some day to explore and trade among them.

During these days, the Indians amused themselves by shaving off part of Pierre's hair in front and arranging it like their own, in the form of a crest on top, adding scarlet string and red paint. One of the Indians gave Pierre a piece of tin used to signal in the sun, to let him see how he looked. Pierre hated being made to appear so like the savages; but he pretended to be delighted. For, if they became angry at him, they might torture or kill him. And, if he pretended to be pleased with what they did, they might grow to like him, and he might have a better chance to escape at some later date.

After two or three days, the Indians allowed Pierre to move about with only one or two guards. Surely, his idea of accepting his fate must be a good one, for one young and well-built Indian paid him special attention, made him understand that he was his owner, and even tried to teach Pierre some of the Mohawk words.

"Ya-le-wah-noh!" said this Indian, pointing to himself.

So Pierre guessed that he was giving his own name; and, when Pierre pointed to the Indian and repeated, "Ya-le-wah-noh!", the Indian grinned delighted at him.

Next, with the forefinger of one hand, Ya-le-wah-noh counted off on the fingers of his other hand. And, seeing that Pierre understood and was trying to follow, Ya-le-wah-noh counted to ten on all his fingers and toes. Over and over, Pierre repeated after him the Indian words, "Onscat, tiggeni, asse, ceyere, wiseh, jayack, tsadack, sategon, tyochte, oyere."

Ya-le-wah-noh seemed so delighted over Pierre's learning that he called other Indians to hear him. And they all smiled and nodded their approval. Pierre began to take heart.

Each day, after the hunting, a great feast was prepared. This fresh meat was more palatable to Pierre than the half-spoiled meat they had given him the first day, and Ya-le-wah-noh saw that he had all he could eat. After the feasting, some of the younger Indians rose and, alternately swaying their bodies backward and forward, they danced and sang. Sometimes, they brought forth some Canadian Indians whom they had taken prisoners. Pierre felt very sorry for these poor wretches, for they were made to dance and sing to entertain their captors. How could they bear to do this, when they knew the only fate in store for them was slow torture and ultimate death or slavery?

Pierre sickened at the thought. He wished he might speak to some of these captives, for they were Algonquins and Hurons from the friendly tribes near Three Rivers. Pierre had learned a little of their language, but he dared not call out to them.

Showing his friendliness could not save these poor creatures; and it might destroy the friendly feeling which Ya-le-wah-noh had shown toward him.

When, after a few days, they started out again, Pierre was still tied hand and foot. It was very uncomfortable; and, just as he was wondering how much longer they would keep him like that, Ya-le-wah-noh unfastened the ropes and gave him a paddle. It was good to be able to move freely again. The sun was bright and Pierre enjoyed paddling along on the blue river. He drew in deep breaths of the fresh, crisp air. If only he were merely going to explore the Indian country, he could have been quite happy. But the awful dread of what the Indians might be holding in store for him, made Pierre's heart heavy.

Although after an hour or two of paddling, Pierre began to grow very tired, he would not let the Indians know how weary he felt, for fear they would think him weak. He knew they abhorred a weakling. So he kept doggedly at it. Perspiration rolled down face, and, at last, he could no longer hide his fatigue. All the other Indians in the canoe laughed; but Ya-le-wah-noh showed him how to use his paddle to save his strength, by relaxing between each stroke. That must be how the Indians could keep at it all day long. Ya-le-wah-noh taught Pierre to sing as they paddled along, and he listened in silence when Pierre sang his French songs.

As they progressed further along the river, they could see an Indian village in the distance. Pierre wondered if they would stop; and, if so, how these Indians might treat him. He was soon to know, for, gradually, they drew nearer and nearer until they could see the barrel-like roofs of the bark-covered houses. When they were almost in to shore, they made Pierre and the other prisoners stand. It was an impressive sight as, having given a few powerful strokes, all the Indians rose, as one man, and, with their paddles held statuesquely aloft, they glided in to shore.

All the villagers crowed around them, and there was much shouting and jubilation over these Indian warriors and their prisoners. Pierre was frightened when one of the village

Indians grasped him, and was about to drag him off, evidently to kill him. He dared not cry out. But Ya-le-wah-noh saw, and interferred. It must be, thought Pierre, they are waiting to take me all the way to their home before they decide what to do with me. The thought did not make him any happier, for he knew that the Indians believed it their sacred duty to exact revenge on all prisoners.

Three days later they reached another Indian camp of about two dozen bark-covered houses. These were set well back from the water so the inhabitants could not be so readily attacked by an enemy approaching in canoes. Here, again, one Indian walked up to Pierre and struck him. He dared not show how much he was hurt. If his life were to be saved, he must show all the courage he could muster. If he could prove himself brave enough, they might not kill him. So, even under this heavy blow, he stood without flinching.

To his surprise, Ya-le-wah-noh then ran to him and motioned that he was to fight. Immediately, the Indians formed a ring, the better to watch the combat.

Pierre fought with every ounce of strength at his command. Into each blow he put an expression of his hatred at being taken captive. Fear of not winning seemed to increase his strength; for he fought like a young tiger. He must gain the good will of his Indian captors by proving to them that he could fight. They were all crowded round, shouting and yelling.

After a time, his fierce blows began to tell. When the young Indian began to realize that he was being beaten, he became very angry, and began to kick. Pierre kicked back. Pierre's shoes of heavy leather with wooden soles could do more damage than the Indian's soft moccasins, and that angered the Indian the more. Grasping Pierre by the wrist, he tried to pull him over. But Pierre was too quick for him. Suddenly, a half-forgotten trick which his father had taught him came to his mind. He watched for an opportunity and, when it came, he speedily caught the young Indian by the wrist and swiftly threw him to the ground and, straddling his prostrate form, punched him until the other Indians pulled him off.

Then there was great jubilation among Pierre's captors. They danced and shouted, making him understand how pleased they were to see him win. Pierre was glad to know that they had seen he could fight. Perhaps they would not torture him so much if they believed he was brave.

Three or four days later, when the Indians were only a short distance from their homes, they stopped once more beside a wide lake. Again, Pierre became worried over what they were going to do. From the place where they had securely bound him, he watched some of the party heat stones red hot. Other Indians were interlacing branches to form shelters over pools of water; and, into these pools they dropped the red-hot stones while great clouds of steam arose. Were they going to smother him and the other prisoners to death?

But, to his surprise, the Indians stripped, and ran, shouting into the steaming shelters. They made great noises while inside, and then, after an hour, Pierre saw them come out, and, still yelling, run to push each other into the lake.

After this cleansing ceremony, they cooked a feast of two bears, and, having eaten their fill, and made sure the prisoners were secure, they settled down to sleep.

Sometime during the night, a sound awakened Pierre. Listening, he could hear shots. If only he knew who it was! Perhaps, after all, he might be rescued. His heart pounded with excitement. If these were white people, perhaps he could escape! But his Indian captors were awakened, also, and they rushed to their canoes. Forcing Pierre to lie down, they paddled so fiercely that by morning they were securely hidden far down the lake in some tall rushes. If it were rescuers Pierre had heard, he knew they could not find him there.

For several days they traveled on this lake. Once, when some deer were spied in the woods near shore, some of the Indians ambushed them and chased them into the water. From the canoes, others shot a few. One very frightened deer swam near the canoe in which Ya-le-wah-noh and Pierre were paddling. Quick as a flash, Ya-le-wah-noh reached out, grasped the startled animal by the horns while he fastened on a bell. Those nearby who saw this watched expectantly. And great was their glee at seeing the rest of the herd almost trampling each other in their frightened attempts to escape from this strange and noisy creature as it strove to hide with them in the woods.

A day later found them paddling down a small river. There was great excitement and jubilation among the savages, as they encamped that night; but Pierre grew more and more troubled. It must be they were nearly home; and the time he had been dreading must be near at hand. If he could talk with someone, it would help. But the few words he had learned from Ya-le-wah-noh were hardly enough to carry on a conversation.

What would they do with him and all the rest of the prisoners? He knew prisoners were always cruelly treated to avenge any of their own warriors who had been killed in battle. And, all winter long, these Indians had been on the warpath, and many of their number had been slain. When Ya-le-wah-noh brought him his supper, he was not hungry; and he did not sleep very well that night.

CHAPTER V

The next morning, Pierre's heart sank as he saw they were approaching a palisaded Indian town. Outside the palisades corn was beginning to grow in cleared areas. Over the top of the palisades, he could see the barrel-like roofs of many houses. Suddenly, there was a great shouting and yelling, and many Indians came rushing from the village to meet them. Pierre was terrified when he saw them crowded together, and armed with sticks, stones, and war clubs. They took a stand, shouting and yelling ominously, as they waited the nearer approach of the warriors and their victims.

Quickly, his Indian captors stripped him and all the other prisoners, while the howling mob from the village formed into two lines close together, each Indian waiting expectantly for his chance to would the prisoners. Pierre knew then that they must all run the gauntlet between these two rows of Indians, or else face death by slow torture. As Ya-le-wah-noh pushed Pierre into the line, and the warriors were motioning them to run as fast as possible, he summoned all his courage. No matter what they did to him, he must not flinch. He took one step forward.

An old woman, and a little boy with a hatchet, stood near the head of the hostile and threatening Indian group. Pierre noticed her startled expression as she gazed at his naked white skin and fair hair so in contrast with the other prisoners. As he was taking another step forward, the old woman, with the little boy by the hand, suddenly broke from the group and came running toward him. Pierre was more terrified than ever. Old women, he knew, had great influence with an Indian tribe. Was he to be singled out for some special torture? What were they going to do with him? Pierre gritted his teeth. But, to his surprise, the old woman threw a blanket around him; and she and the boy led him inside the stockade past several bark-covered cabins, and over to one near the center of the village. Motioning encouragingly to him, the old woman and

37

the boy led him inside. After the bright morning sun, it seemed very dark inside the cabin; but Pierre could see the old woman leaning over a pot and extracting some pieces of meat with her fingers. While the little boy watched curiously, she offered these to Pierre, but, though he tried, he was so frightened he could not swallow.

For about an hour, the old woman and the little boy sat gaping at Pierre. Outside, he could hear excited jabbering and shouting, and he shuddered as he pictured to himself the probable tortures which were being inflicted on the rest of the prisoners. Were they reserving some special torment for him because he was a white boy?

At last, he heard a slight sound behind him, and, daring to turn his head, he beheld a company of old Indian men filing quietly into the cabin. Their moccasins made no sound as they circled the dirt floor of the cabin. In complete silence, they took up positions, cross-legged on the floor, and, for what seemed an eternity to Pierre, smoked, and occasionally glanced in his direction.

Just when Pierre was thinking he could stand the suspense no longer, these men rose, and, as silently as they had entered, they raised him to his feet and took him to another, larger bark-covered cabin in the center of the village. Here, Pierre found more blanketed men sitting cross-legged in a circle, and all smoking together. A fire burned brightly in the center of the dirt floor, and they made Pierre sit close to it . Were they going to torture him by fire? Complete silence filled the cabin. How long would they make him wait? While he was wondering, the old woman appeared. Pierre watched her, anxiously, as she stood before the quietly smoking men and made a speech in a very loud voice. When she had finished, all the Indians took their pipes from their mouths and shouted, "Hoh! Hoh!" By this, Pierre knew that they all agreed to whatever she had said. Was she pleading for him? While the men remained quietly smoking, she removed her wampum belt. Then she tied it around Pierre and led him back to her own cabin.

When she seated him in the place of honor, Pierre was greatly relieved. It must be she had really saved him from being tortured. Next, he was amazed to see her dance and sing a little. Then, calling to an Indian girl, she gave her a comb. and the girl began to comb Pierre's hair. They did not seem to be able to do enough for him. They washed the paint off his face, fed him, and gave him some Indian clothing — a blue blanket, mocassins, and buckskin for leggings.

For the first time in all the horrible and anxious weeks since his capture, Pierre began to feel comfortable. Taking courage, he looked about the long, narrow cabin. By the light which shone in at the door at each end, he saw that the frame work was of medium-sized poles bound together with thongs of wood fibre, and covered on the outside with huge slabs of bark. There was no furniture, but, against the walls, in several places, raised boards had been fastened, and, over these, animal skins had been thrown. Pierre guessed these must be the family's beds, especially since small piles of rushes placed at one end would seem to serve as pillows. There were bows and arrows, and personal belongings, too, but Pierre had no more time to look at these, for the old woman and the girl were trying to help him put on his new clothing.

Pierre felt very self-conscious when they stepped back to admire his changed appearance; and he noted with gratitude, the smile of admiration on the round face of the older woman, and the long, slender face of the girl. He had time, now, to really look at them as they stood there. Both were clothed in loose deerskin garments and moccasins, and their long, black hair, tied at the nape of the neck, hung down their backs. The older woman was short and stout, her good-natured, weathered face and her work-worn hands testifying to her useful life. But the young girl was straight and slender, the skin of her face smooth, and her dark eyes under long lashes beamed friendliness as she smiled at Pierre.

He wished he could talk with them to learn what this was all about. Smiling back at them, he attempted a few of the words that Ya-le-wah-noh had taught him. Pointing to them. and then to himself, he pronounced the word "Rocktse", meaning friends. The old woman and the girl opened their eyes in amazement, and began jabbering excitedly at him. But, Pierre was at a total loss to know what they were saying, and he was forced to shake his head and shrug his shoulders. Then, all three of them laughed together. How good it was to feel that he had some friends once more!

Suddenly it occurred to him that these Indians might be able to understand the Huron language, which he had learned to speak fairly well back at Three Rivers. As he pronounced the first few words, a puzzled expression crept over the girl's face. But the old woman's lit up with excitement and joy. Not waiting for him to finish, she began talking.

"My name Ga-nonk-we'-non," she said. "I was of the Huron, but now I am Mohawk. My son, Orihma, was killed in battle. You are now my son, Orimha."

Pierre remembered having heard of this Indian custom of adopting a prisoner to take the place of a son killed in battle. So that was it!

Pierre repeated, "Orimha," and the old woman smiled at him. Then, taking the girl by the hand, she continued. "This is one of your new sisters, Conharraffan, and the other is A-we-not. Your new brother, Hoh-squa-sa-ga-deh, is hunting. Your new father, Arenias, is a mighty and brave chief. He comes now."

Pierre turned just as a figure blotted out the light from the doorway. A tall well-formed Indian, clad only in breech clout and moccasins, was entering. His hair was cut in the usual manner of the Mohawk warriors, with one long lock hanging down on either side of his head, and, on top, a streak of hair cut like a crest and extending from his forehead to his neck, all the hair next to it on either side being cut off. As he advanced into the cabin, Arenias gave no sign of surprise at seeing Pierre there; but, silently getting some tobacco and a pipe, he prepared for a smoke. It was Ga-nonk-we'-non who broke the silence, chattering quickly in the Mohawk tongue to this stern-faced and self-composed man.

When she had finished, he removed his pipe only long enough to say "hoh!" and then sat down on the floor and enjoyed his smoke. Pierre admired not only his dignity, but the quiet strength of the man as his muscles rippled with any slight change of position, and he gazed with awe at the nineteen marks on his thigh. Those, he knew, meant that this man had, single-handed, killed that many enemies in battle. He must, indeed, be a strong and brave man!

Just then, Pierre's new mother indicated that he was to sit down, too. The women brought food which the men ate. Afterward, the women sat by themselves and had their supper.

Pierre longed to ask questions, but, deciding the time was not appropriate, he, also, maintained a silence. ·After a time, Pierre's new father filled his pipe and smoked again, and, the sun having begun to set, his mother pointed out a bed for Pierre.

Almost contently, he settled down. For, now, even as he had planned, if his life were spared, he could learn the Mohawk language, and their ways of living; he would make friends with them. And, some day, having made his escape, he would come back with other Frenchmen to explore and trade. For the first time in many a night, Pierre drifted off to sleep, untroubled by terrified thoughts of what fate the dawn might be holding in store for him.

CHAPTER VI

In the days which followed, Pierre spent all of his waking moments exploring the Indian village, becoming acquainted with the people and trying to learn their language and their customs.

He was interested to note that there were about sixty bark-covered houses in the village, and that in the center was the council house, or Long House where he had been taken on the first day of judgment. He shuddered to himself as he walked as quickly as possible past the scaffolds which had been erected for the express purpose of torturing prisoners. How grateful he was that he had been spared this agony!

Surrounding the village were two rows of palisades made of sharply-pointed sticks placed upright, side by side. The two gates at the east and the west ends were guarded by three huge wooden images carved like men; and Pierre shivered a little as he realized that the objects fluttering from these entrances were dried scalps, hanging by the scalp lock. One of them might have been his!

Outside the stockade were cleared lands where the Indians raised their crops. Pierre watched the women and girls preparing the land and planting corn, squash, and beans. He saw where tobacco and fruit were grown and he marvelled at the quantities of food raised with only crude instruments for doing the work.

As he explored outside the stockade, he was curious about some palisades here and there, the red, white, and blue-painted logs so close together there was no possible opening anywhere. Only one larger one had an opening at the top, and this was partly covered over with a huge, wooden bird, while round the sides were painted dogs, deer, snakes, and other beasts.

Going back to the village, he found his new mother pounding corn, and he learned from her that these small palisades contained graves, and that the one with the animal paintings and carved bird was that of a chief.

Everywhere Pierre went, he was showered with kindnesses and often presented with gifts. The women and children marveled at his white skin, his fair hair, and his blue eyes, and he came to enjoy all these attentions which were paid him.

He was invited into many of the bark-covered cabins. Some were small, but many were large enough to accommodate several families, each one of which had its own section and its own opening in the roof so fires could be built on the dirt floor below and the smoke would rise through these holes.

Week by week, as Pierre became a little more familiar with the language, and grew better acquainted with these Indians, he admired their skills and their organized living.

Ya-le-wah-noh often came to take him through the village, and to help him talk with the other Indians. He showed Pierre the storehouse of food. There was one in which a hundred or more dried salmon hung, and bags and bags called "notasten" made from plaited hemp in which had been placed dried eels. More food was stored in barrels made of bark fastened together with thongs of the inner bark of the elm. And he showed Pierre vast pits into which last year's corn, corn from the cob, had been preserved all winter. In some cabins were forty or fifty deer cut in quarters and dried. And, fastened in one corner of the stockade was a bear which was being fattened for butchering.

Often Pierre watched the Indian women sitting on the ground outside their cabin doors working at their daily tasks. Some made meal by dropping kernels of corn into a hollowed piece of log and pounding it with a pole-like stick which had been made thinner in the middle. Some fashioned moccasins of deerskin or braided corn husks; others shaped damp clay into bowls and pipes. Pierre was interested in watching their deft fingers scrape and press designs into the pottery, and shape animal decorations on the bowls of the pipes. These decorations were always so placed that the smoker could see them while enjoying his pipe of tobacco. Some women prepared tinder for lighting fires by shredding dry bark and mixing it with powder-dry grass. Pierre was fascinated to see the Indians laboriously shaping shells into small cyclindrical forms, and boring a hole through the center. This was their money, called wampum, or seawan, and the wealthy of the tribe owned great belts and strings of it. Many times Pierre's new friends presented some to him.

One task which the women were not allowed to perform was the making of the large nets or seines for fishing. Ten or twelve men owned each of these in common and they all went together to use them. When Pierre asked Ya-le-wah-noh why the women did not make these, he replied that if they did, the fish would know and would not come near the nets.

One morning after breakfast, his foster mother called him to her and said,

"Your new father makes a great feast for you to show that you are his son. He asks many warriors. Chagon!" (which meant, "Be happy!")

Pierre did feel quite happy. And why not? Had not the Indians shown him every consideration? Did he not have a very easy life among them? His new mother and his sisters took every care of him, and waited on him hand and foot. His father gave him gifts, his brother took him fishing and hunting; and, everywhere he went, he was welcomed by all. For what more could he wish? Except, of course, to get back home. But he must wait, and not think of that now.

Pierre was greatly interested in the preparations for the feast. From their magnitude, he could not doubt that they were to be worthy of a celebration in honor of a chief's son. He watched the women preparing great quantities of meat and beating corn into small pieces between two stones, and baking cakes from it in the ashes.

At last the great day dawned, and Pierre's two sisters washed him and greased his hair. His mother dressed him with two necklaces of porcelain shells. Next, his brother painted his face, and tied porcelain shells to his two locks of hair. But his foster father was not satisfied with Pierre's blue cap. He replaced it with a garland, and added another necklace of porcelain, or wampum which hung to Pierre's heels; and he gave him a hatchet.

Pierre was so laden with the weight of all these riches that he could not have defended himself with the hatchet, if such a thing had been necessary. But he began to feel very important; and, bedecked as he was, he had to walk very slowly, and with great dignity.

When he and his father came out of the cabin, Pierre was both astonished and pleased at the great shouts of welcome from the throats of the several hundred men gathered for the feast. His father seated him, and motioned for all the others to sit down. Standing erectly with his arms folded across his chest, he waited for the group to become quiet. Then, raising his head, he threw out the tones of his voice across the heads of all those assembled, so that everyone could hear, clearly, what he had to say. And, as he talked, his voice grew louder and louder until it reached a mighty crescendo, like a roar.

"To-day, I give thee my son, Orimha. No more is he French. From today, he is Mohawk! He is strong and brave; he can fight like a Mohawk!"

As with one voice, the assembled group shouted a mighty, "Hoh!"

Arenias continued, speaking ever louder and louder. He told of the glories of his people; of their heroes; of their deeds. More and more often, his fascinated audience chanted, "Hoh, Hoh!" in approval of this fine oration. At last, Arenias smote his chest with one fist and shouted, "Ihy othkon! Tkoschs ko, aguweechon Kajingahaga kouaane Jountuck! Cha Othkok!" which meant, "I am the devil! Really, all the Mohawks are very cunning devils!"

Then, seizing a hatchet, with one mighty blow, he struck and broke open a kettle of cagamite which was made of corn meal boiled with bits of fish or meat. Raising the hatchet with one hand, and lifting Pierre to his feet with the other, he shouted, "This is my son, Orimha! I break the kettle to show he is man of valor, thirsting for the blood of his enemies!"

45

Then, a great shouting and tumult arose. There were cries of "Hoh! Hoh!" and "Chagon, Orimha!" which meant, "Be hearty! Be happy!"

When at last they were quieted down, and seated for the feast, Pierre felt very proud of his father's oratory; and of his acceptance into the tribe. This was indeed an honor! And he was very proud of his new and rich finery, too.

Young boys were bringing in the steaming kettles of food. How good it was! There were kettles of moose, beaver, deer, and corn meal flavored with bears' grease. There were turkey, and beans cooked with bear bacon, and fish, and turtle, and corn cakes, and corn bread baked with dried strawberries, nuts, cherries, and sun flower seeds. Pierre thought he had never seen such a feast. Glancing round at all these Indians, he thought how glad he was to be feasting with them instead of having them dance with his scalp on a pole.

As the guests became too full to eat any more, they began to dance and sing. Soon more and more joined in, all singing, and some shouting, "Netho! Netho!" which meant, "It is well!"

For a long time this singing and dancing and shouting continued. Then, at last, the celebration ceased, and the departing guests called "Chagon, Orimha!" meaning "Be happy, Orimha! Be hearty!"

If Pierre's chest swelled a little with pride that night, who could blame him? Now, he was one of them! Now he could come and go as he pleased. He had succeeded in one part of his purpose. Perhaps, some day, he could fulfill the rest of his desires.

The next morning, Ya-le-wah-noh came to him.

"Now you are a true Mohawk; come with me. We go to the cabin of Ho'-sa-ho-ho. For a long time, he has a devil. We go to drive it away."

By this, Pierre knew that Ho'-sa-ho-ho was sick; and that he was not only to be allowed to see this ceremony of driving out the devil, but to help as well.

Halfway across the village, they joined a band of some ten or eleven men, mostly old. Their faces were painted red, and, having welcomed Ya-le-wah-noh and Pierre, they waited while they smeared paint on their faces. Three of the men had on their heads wreaths of deer hair into which had been braided pieces of some kind of green herb; and stuck through with five white cross-like forms. As they entered the cabin of Ho'-sa-ho-ho, Pierre watched carefully in order to do exactly what the other Indians were doing.

First, some covered the dirt floor thickly with the bark of trees, while the rest carried Ho'-sa-ho-ho and placed him on the floor in the center of the cabin. An old woman who had been quietly waiting, moved silently over to his side and raised a turtle shell rattle which had been made by placing many beads inside the empty shell.

When the men had finished spreading the bark, she began to clink the turtle shell rattle, and all began to sing to its rhythm. Pierre did not know this song, but he caught a word here and there, and he followed the motions of the rest as they pretended to catch the devil and trample him to death.

Faster and faster they ran and stamped; and faster and faster the old woman beat out the rhythm of the song, as they trampled the bark to atoms. When, at last, little clouds of dust arose, the Indians appeared afraid; and they blew it at each other, and ran as if they were really afraid it might be the devil.

Just as Pierre was becoming so tired it seemed as if he would have to stop, one old man went up to Ho'-sa-ho-ho and took from his hands a dead otter which the sick man had been holding. Next, the old man placed his mouth on the back of Ho'sa-ho-ho's neck and sucked hard, after which he spat in the otter's mouth, and, throwing the animal to the floor, he ran off as if pursued. From then on Pierre was amazed to see others go to the otter, and then work themselves into a perfect frenzy. They began to throw and seemingly catch fire, scattering red-hot coal and ashes about the cabin floor.

Pierre had great doubts as to the success of this treatment, and he was very glad when Ya-le-wah-noh started for the cabin door and he knew he would be able to leave without

47

offending anyone.

On days when it was stormy, Pierre had a chance to visit with his foster father. This was a good opportunity to learn more about the people of his foster father's tribe.

"Who are the Mohawk people?" he asked.

His father seemed pleased at his question.

"We are the Keepers of the Eastern Door", he answered. "We belong with our Brothers, the Oneidas, the Onondagas, the Senecas, and the Cayugas; and all our lands together are a great Nation. We are like one family in a huge Long House. The Oneidas are the People of the Stone, for they possess a sacred stone which they brought from a land far away; the Onondagas are the People of the Mountains and the Keepers of the Council Fires, for it is here that we often hold our councils. The Cayugas are our youngest brothers. The Senecas are the Keepers of the Western Door."

Pierre thought for a moment.

"Why do you carry a tortoise when you go on the warpath?"

His father raised one hand and shook his forefinger at Pierre.

"Never forget this, my son. We are the Turtle Tribe of the Mohawks. There are also the Bear Tribe and the Wolf Tribe."

He pounded his chest.

"But we are the Turtle! If I take a turtle on the warpath, that makes me the very devil so I cannot be hurt. Of all the Mohawks, the Turtle Tribe is the greatest."

He raised his head proudly. "We are descended from the Woman of Creation who fell out of the Heavens. There was no earth then — just water. But when the woman fell, she fell onto a turtle's back. With her hands, she paddled. And as she paddled, she scooped up earth until finally the world was made. She is our ancestor, my son. Do not ever forget. We are the Tortoise Tribe — the greatest of the Mohawks!

And, of all the Iroquois, the Mohawks are the fiercest fighters. Do not forget this, my son. Always be brave!"

"I will remember," replied Pierre.

CHAPTER VII

Several days after the feast, when Pierre had begun to feel very restless, he wanderd into the woods. As he walked aimlessly about, thinking of his home back in Three Rivers, he heard a slight sound. Glancing about, he saw an Indian boy coming through the forest; and then another, and another. They called to him, "Orimha! Orimha!" and he saw they were three of his acquaintances, Sa-ha-whe, Ha-ie-no-nis, and Ro-heh-hon.

"We are going hunting," said Sa-ha-whe. "Why do you not come with us?"

The idea made Pierre happy, but he hestitated, for he still had not entirely rid himself of the idea that he was being watched.

"Do you think they would let me?" he asked.

Ha-ie-no-nis stepped forward.

"I will go with you while you ask your mother."

Quickly the two boys hurried through the woods and back to the village. When they came to Pierre's cabin, he stood before his mother.

"My mother," he said, "I have learned many Indian ways. I know how to walk like an Indian; I can dance and sing, and speak many Mohawk words. No longer am I French. I am Mohawk. Now, I would like to go hunting to prove I am a real man."

His mother looked quietly up at him. Thinking she might refuse Ha-ie-no-nis stepped forward.

"Two of my friends go, also. We would show him how to look after himself."

His mother thought for a moment. Then, "You may go," she replied. "Come, I will give you food and hunting material."

She brought him a musket, three pairs of moccasins, and a sack of meal. As Pierre was about to pick them up, she called to her two daughters, "Take these for your brother; and carry them into the woods for him. He goes to hunt with his friends."

Obediently, Conharraffen and A-we-not took up Pierre's musket, food, and extra clothing; and, with Ha-ie-no-nis, they went back to the woods to find Ro-heh-hon and Sa-ha-whe who had been left there.

"Good," they said when they saw Pierre and his sisters coming. "Now we will show you how an Indian hunts. We go this way."

After a while Conharraffen and A-we-not stopped.

"We go back, now," they said, and left.

So Pierre was forced to carry his own belongings. This was not as much fun as he had thought it was going to be, for it was hot traveling, and they had hardly stopped to rest. The mosquitoes were very annoying; and they had seen no game. Pierre began to wish he had stayed at home.

After two days they reached a river, where his companions halted. They began to cut down a tree, and Pierre was amazed to see them peel off the bark, and make a canoe in less than two hours. The canoe was not very large, but they all managed to squeeze into it.

"This is much better," said Pierre to himself, as they paddled along. "Even if it is crowded, it is easier than walking all the time."

As if he knew what Pierre was thinking, Sa-ha-whe turned toward him and said, "You get tired, my brother?"

Afraid they might think him a weakling, Pierre hastened to answer, "Na, I am all right."

Sa-ha-whe smiled.

"Soon we will find some game, and then we will have fresh meat to eat."

Just then, there was a crackling in the bushes along the shore. Turning, Pierre saw a huge bear; but before he could aim his musket, Ro-heh-hon had shot him. When he saw how disappointed Pierre was, Ro-heh-hon said, "We will let you shoot the next time." And Pierre was pleased.

50

By the close of that day, they had killed three bears, a deer, and a beaver; and, before rolling up their blankets and going to sleep, they had a great feast.

When morning came, Ha-ie-no-nis said, "Let us set traps today. Then we can start back home, and come later to see what is caught."

So Pierre helped with the traps, and, as they were starting back, they all suddenly realized that someone was singing.

"Hide!" whispered Sa-ha-whe. Pierre crouched behind a large tree trunk. Surely this could be no enemy when he was letting himself be heard. Nevertheless, he peaked out cautiously, and soon saw a lone Indian coming toward them.

When Pierre's companions sighted him, they stepped from their hiding places.

"He is all right. We know him!" called Sa-ha-whe. "He is a friend called Te-cum-seh." And they all greeted the Indian.

Pierre had never seen Te-cum-seh before, but he understood why not when Te-cum-seh said he had come from the land of the Oneidas, and had been hunting with them.

That evening, while the meat was boiling, Te-sum-seh came and sat close to Pierre. For a few moments he was silent; and then, in a low tone, he began to speak in the Algonquin tongue. Pierre was startled, and he felt a pang of homesickness; for this was the language of the friendly Indians who lived near his home at Three Rivers.

Te-cum-seh smiled at the show of surprise on Pierre's face. He continued to speak in a low tone.

"I am Algonquin. Many moons ago these Mohawks captured and brought me to their Long House. They tortured me and kept me prisoner. But they do not watch me, now. His searching eyes flashed. "Tell me are you French?"

Fearful that the boys would hear, Pierre dared only to nod his head, but how his heart was pounding at these reminders of home!

As if he knew Perre's thoughts, Te-cum-seh was continuing.

51

"Tell me of Three Rivers. Near there was my home. Do you not wish to be back there?"

As if a hand had suddenly clutched him about the throat, Pierre felt as if he were being strangled. Hot tears welled up into his eyes, and he blinked rapidly to dry them.

Te-cum-seh moved closer.

"Do you like the Mohawks?"

Pierre did not know what to say. This Indian might just be trying to get him to complain, so he could tell the others.

Therefore, he merely replied, "They are good to me." Te-cum-seh's voice became tense, "Let us escape to Three Rivers!" Pierre did not reply.

Te-cum-seh persisted; but Pierre answered by saying that the boys had promised to bring him back to his Indian mother.

Te-cum-seh pressed closer to Pierre.

"Do you not love the French? Do you not wish to see your own people; to be free; and to eat French bread once more?"

Pierre could not help the look of longing which came across his face. Seeing it, Te-cum-seh continued, "Brother, take courage! Let us get away! Three Rivers is not far off."

At these words, Pierre's heart leaped. Perhaps this was his chance. But before Pierre could answer, Sa-ha-whe called to them, "What do you two talk about?"

Pierre was troubled. What if they had heard and understood all that Te-cum-seh had said? He called out, "We just talk." Pierre breathed easier when they seemed satisfied, and went on with their cooking.

Under his breath Te-cum-seh whispered, "Together we could escape. It will be easy. While they are asleep, we will kill them with their own hatchets."

At the thought of this, Pierre drew away.

When he did not seem to agree, Te-cum-seh continued, "Do not hestitate, my friend. Even if they have been good to you, think how many of your own people they have killed. They are cruel. How do you know if they will continue to be kind to you? Anyway, would you not rather be back at Three Rivers again?"

Suddenly Pierre became so homesick he could hardly stand it. Visions of home, and his own people rose before him. He could see his mother and father and his sister Margaret. What did they think had become of him? To be sure, these these Indians had been good to him. But would it last? If, at any time, he failed to please them, they might make him a slave, or torture, or kill him. Just as Te-cum-seh had said, was he to spend all his days in captivity? Here was the chance for which he had been longing. He would have help to escape. This chance might never come again; but could he trust this Algonquin?

Just then, Ro-heh-hon called them to supper. All the time they were eating, Pierre kept thinking of what Te-cum-seh had said.

Later, when they had rolled themselves up in their blankets, Te-cum-seh pulled himself over to Pierre and whispered in his ear, "You will come, my friend? We are not far from Three Rivers. It is your one good chance, for you could never find your way alone. See, they do not keep their weapons beside them. That will make it easy. Would you not like to be home again?"

Pierre could stand it no longer. He thought of all the cruel deeds these Indians had done; of all the French people they had killed and tortured — the French, his own countrymen. How could he go on living with such cruel savages? Again a vision of his family rose before his eyes, his mother, his father, and Margaret in their comfortable cabin. Suddenly, an overwhelming desire to get home seized him. No matter what the cost, he must get there.

"Yes," he whispered fiercely. "Yes, I'll go!"

"Good!" replied Te-cum-seh. "We will wait until they are asleep."

And he rolled over and calmly settled down as if to go to sleep, himself. But Pierre could not even close his eyes. His heart pounded with excitement. He was not cold, but he shivered under his blanket.

CHAPTER VIII

After what seemed hours, Te-cum-seh touched Pierre on the shoulder and quietly handed him a hatchet. Softly, Te-cum-seh crept toward the soundly sleeping boys. As Pierre saw him raise his hatchet above Sa-ha-whe's head, he was suddenly sickened and ashamed. Even if these Indians had killed his own people, they had treated him well. How could he allow such a thing to happen to them? He would stop Te-cum-seh. But, even as he ran toward him, he saw it was too late; for, in the moonlight, he could discern that Te-cum-seh had already killed Sa-ha-whe and was standing over Ha-ie-no-nis.

Frozen with horror at the sight, he stood helplessly while Te-cum-seh finished the horrible deed. He was nauseated while he watched Te-cum-seh scalp the two boys. Pierre turned away from the bloody sight. Not only did he feel sick, but he was dazed. Surely, this could not be true! It must all be happening in a dream. Te-cum-seh touched him on the shoulder.

"Why do you not help?" he asked. When Pierre did not reply, he continued, "We will take their muskets and some food and go in their canoe," and he pushed Pierre toward the water.

Mechanically, Pierre stepped into the canoe and they paddled off. He felt numbed and frightened. He should not have allowed these murders to take place. But then how else could he ever escape? For he could never find his way alone; and, if Te-cum-seh had not slain the boys, they would have followed them, and tortured, or perhaps killed them for trying to escape. Pierre kept turning these thoughts over and over in his mind as they paddled all through the night.

After what seemed endless hours, Te-cum-seh broke the silence.

"Dawn will soon come, my brother. Let us stop by some rocks. Water and rocks leave no trail. If we leave no tracks, we can not be followed.

"I see," was all Pierre replied.

In a few moments Te-cum-seh touched him on the shoulder.

"We go in here," he said. "Here are some good rocks."

Pierre helped him drag the canoe over the rocks and into the woods. When they had reached a secluded spot, Te-cum-seh halted.

"Here is a good place. We will turn the canoe over. Then, after we have eaten, we will crawl under it and sleep."

Te-cum-seh ate heartily, but Pierre was not very hungry. Nor did he sleep very well after they had lain down under the canoe. The thought of those three scalps dangling from Te-cum-seh's belt made him feel sick. It was raining by now, and the mosquitoes were biting in such great numbers, he could hardly lie still.

But evidently neither rain nor thoughts, nor mosquitoes disturbed Te-cum-seh, for he slept soundly.

Pierre lay, cramped and miserable, watching the day break and grow brighter and brighter.

Some hours later, when nightfall had come, and Te-cum-seh stirred, Pierred crawled out from under the canoe. Te-cum-seh was soon out, too. Half playfully, he shook Pierre by the shoulder.

"Take heart, my brother," he said. "They will not start to look for us yet. I know my way through these woods, and we can be nearly home before they begin to ask why you do not return."

Pierre made no reply.

"Come," Te-cum-seh said. We will eat. Then you will feel better, my friend. Soon it will be quite dark, and we can set out once more. We will travel by night, when we can not be seen; and we will sleep, hidden in the woods, by day. You will see how it can be done."

Pierre ate very little and his heart was still heavy as they embarked. They did not dare to talk for fear of being heard by some chance band of Indians. As they paddled silently on, hour after hour, in the fearsome darkness, Pierre strained every nerve to listen for what might be the approach of an enemy. Even as their powerful paddling shot them swiftly forward into the unknown blackness, Pierre dreaded the unseen dangers which his staring eyes could not see. Were they really heading for Three Rivers? Twice during the night, Te-cum-seh touched Pierre and pointed to the shore where a small fire was burning among the dense woods. Each time, they both stopped paddling, and Pierre held his breath while they floated past in hushed silence. What if a keen Indian ear should have heard their dipping paddles?

For two weeks Pierre and Te-cum-seh traveled after dark, sleeping hidden in the forest by day. But even though he was very tired every night, Pierre did not sleep soundly; and he shivered when, huddled behind trees and underbrush, they could hear canoes paddling by in broad daylight.

One night, after they had paddled for several hours, Te-cum-seh steered their canoe to shore.

"Let us rest for a while," he whispered. "Then, when it grows light, we will see where we are."

As quietly as they could, they pulled the canoe into the thick woods and hid. When daylight arrived at last, Te-cum-seh was jubilant.

"Look!" he cried. "We are almost there. Look! Look!" and he pointed across the river.

After all the weary days and nights, Pierre could hardly believe it. "Are we really?" he asked.

"Yes! Yes! See? We cross the great river and go a short way, and we are at Three Rivers!"

For the first time since they had set out, Pierre began to feel better.

"If only we can cross without being caught!"

"I will take you. Te-cum-seh knows the way," he said as he gazed out over the vast expanse of water shimmering in the bright sun.

Pierre was terrified at such boldness.

Oh no!" he cried. "We have come so far, safely. Let us not try to go in the daylight when we can be seen. Those Indians have probably missed me by now. They may have found our dead companions; they would know I would want to get home; and they will be coming to Three Rivers to look for me. We should wait for darkness, when they can not see us."

But Te-cum-seh could not be persuaded. The nearness of his goal seemed to destroy all caution for him.

"It is two winters since I have seen my people. When we are so close, why do we wait? Let us shake off the yoke of that pack of wolves who have killed so many French people, and so many of my tribe."

Pierre, too, was anxious to reach home, but, "Is it wise?" he asked. "Surely, if there are any Indians out there on the water, they would see us from a long way off. There would be many in each war canoe, and they would go so much faster than we that we could never hope to escape."

Te-cum-seh taunted him.

"You are afraid!" He laughed. "Then I will go by myself, and leave you here. I will tell your French governor at Three Rivers that you stayed hidden like a coward. I go, my brother." And he started toward the canoe.

Pierre was terrified at the thought of being left alone. He was not too sure of the way; and how could he ever cross the river if Te-cum-seh took the canoe? Even now, his Indian enemies might be close at their heels; and he could never hope to escape alone. As Te-cum-seh reached the canoe, Pierre called out, "Wait! I will go. I still think we should hide till night; but I will go with you."

"Good!" replied Te-cum-seh.

As quietly as possible, they set out once more. This part of the great river was very wide, and Pierre gazed across the quiet blue expanse of the water to the distant shore.

For some time they paddled, Pierre ever on the lookout for any danger. Suddenly, his fingers gripped the paddle.

"Look!" he cried.

Te-cum-seh turned his head.

"Where?" he asked.

"There! See that shadow. It moves, sometimes up, sometimes down."

Te-cum-seh stood up in the canoe. For what seemed an eternity, he remained, gazing intently, his hands cupped over his eyes. Then abruptly, he laughed.

"It is only some wild geese, my brother — a whole flock. It is their wings you see going up and down." And Te-cum-seh sat down and continued paddling.

Pierre kept at it, too, but he could not take his eyes from that silently moving shadow. Was it really some geese? He kept his eyes on it as it drew nearer and ever nearer, and seemed to grow larger and larger; and all the time a great dread was welling up within him. As it came ever nearer and nearer, the shadow was changing. Suddenly his hands seemed to freeze onto the paddle. These were no geese! This was an Indian war canoe filled with braves!

Pierre was so frightened he had no breath left to shout a warning. But Te-cum-seh had seen, too, and they both bent every effort to fierce paddling. Harder and harder they paddled; but nearer and nearer came the war canoes. How could they hope to outpaddle so many?

"Turn back to the shore!" panted Te-cum-seh. "We can hide in the forest! Hurry! They are Mohawks!"

CHAPTER IX

Pierre needed no urging. The Mohawks were shouting and yelling as they swept closer and closer. Pierre dared not take time to look around; for shots were hitting the water nearby. Straight ahead were some rushes. If only they could reach them and hide! Pierre glanced down at the water. He could begin to see the bottom; but it was still too deep to wade.

The shouting and yelling was getting closer. A shot sang by his head, and Pierre tried to redouble his efforts. His arms ached so that it seemed as if he could paddle no further. But he must! It was not far to the rushes; perhaps they could reach them.

Suddenly, there was a mighty howl and an angry roar from the pursuing Indians. Pierre looked back. Two Indians in the nearest war canoe were holding something aloft; and Pierre was horrified to see they were the scalps of their former companions. It must be that Te-cum-seh had thrown them into the water and they had floated toward the Mohawks, who had recognized that the scalps were of their tribe.

"Hurry! Hurry!" gasped Te-cum-seh. "The scalps did not sink! Now they know! Hurry! Hurry!"

But before Pierre could turn back to his paddling, Te-cum-seh slumped forward, fatally shot. Pierre struggled to keep the canoe from upsetting, at the same time attempting to duck the fast flying shots. Suddenly, there was water in the canoe Some of the shots must have pierced it!

"I must keep on paddling," thought Pierre. But the canoe was filling rapidly. Just as it sank, the Mohawks reached him and dragged him ashore.

Pierre was so exhausted he could hardly stand. Would they kill him at once, as they had Te-cum-seh? But when they had stripped him, put a halter round his neck, and tied his arms behind his back, he knew he was to be kept as a prisoner. If only some of these Indians might recognize him, perhaps they would not be so cruel.

He tried to see if any of them were from his own village; but there was none he had seen before. There was nothing he could do. He would have to endure whatever revenge they might exact from him, and, when one warrior grasped his hand and chewed out one of his finger nails, Pierre began to truly realize what this might mean. He shut his eyes and gritted his teeth, the better to endure the pain. The pain became more tolerable; he glanced about once more. There were other prisoners, too — three Frenchmen and some Huron Indians who must have come from near Quebec. One of the Frenchmen was tied near Pierre.

"I am Pierre Radisson. Do you know my ——," he began. But an Indian struck him across the mouth so hard that the blood ran, and the Frenchman shook his head in warning.

During the long journey back to the land of the Mohawks, Pierre tried to help his cause by talking to the Indians in the Mohawk tongue.

"I am one of you," he said. And, when they did not answer, "My name is Orimha. My father is a chief; you will see."

But the Indians would not listen. Some of them, even spat on him; and Pierre felt more hopeless every day.

Each night, he and the other prisoners were stripped, thrown to the ground, and fastened to posts driven in the earth. And, with knees, elbows, wrists, and even their hair tied, they could not move even so much as to brush off the myriads of mosquitoes from their naked bodies. Their only relief was to puff and blow their breath in an almost futile effort to scare off a few of these insects.

But, although the nights were terrible, Pierre came to dread some of the days even more. For, whenever they came to an Indian village, all the inhabitants rushed out to torture them by beating, cutting, or burning them or tearing out their finger nails. And the thought of even worse suffering which awaited them at their journey's end, made Pierre feel quite hopeless.

At last, the day which Pierre had dreaded for so long came, and they arrived at the village from which he had escaped. How familiar the stockade looked with its wooden images over the gateway! The villagers were pouring through this entrance, and, with weapons in hand, were readying themselves to maltreat the prisoners.

Pierre gathered his courage as best he could. If he could suffer all the tortures without flinching, he felt hopeful these former friends might spare his life. For, to suffer without showing it, was the Indian ideal. He gritted his teeth as he saw the Indians forming into two rows, for he knew this meant running the gauntlet. Where were his foster father and mother? Would they help him; or would they, too, torture and torment him?

Some of the Indians were lining him up with the other prisoners. Now they were tying them all together by their necks — but leaving their legs free. Pierre knew what that meant! An Indian, pulling on this rope would lead the line down the gauntlet, jerking and yanking them so they would fall; and the Indians would laugh. Then, before the prisoners could get up and run, they would strike them, cruelly. Pierre knew; for he had seen how prisoners were treated by these savages.

The Indians were pushing and pulling now at the line of prisoners. Pierre knew his great ordeal was about to begin; and he was terrified. Just then, he caught sight of his foster father and mother, and brother, and sisters in the crowd. His foster mother saw him at the same time, and she ran to him shouting, "Orimha! Orimha! My son!" and she pulled him from the line.

"My mother!" gasped Pierre.

But she could say no more, for his foster father grasped him by the arm and hurried him toward his former home. Once inside the familiar cabin, he pushed Pierre into a sitting position on the dirt floor. Pierre's heart was pounding with suppressed excitement. Could his father save him from the awful vengeance of these savages? And, if he could, would he? He looked very angry as he glared down at Pierre.

61

"Fool!" he shouted. "Once you were my son. Now you have killed my people; you have made yourself my enemy."

Pierre hung his head. For some moments his Indian father stood staring ahead, his mouth set in a straight line. Then he turned to Pierre's sisters.

"Give him food," he said. "We will see."

Pierre's heart nearly choked him. Did this mean his father would try to save him; or would special punishment be dealt out to him because he, a chief's adopted son, had laid hands on his people?

Pierre's sisters tried to smile at him, but that made him feel no better. He took the food they brought and managed to swallow most of it. If he were to be tortured, he would need something to increase his strength. Everyone was silent while he ate, and Pierre looked from one expressionless face to the other, but found no comfort there. From outside he could hear the commotion as the other prisoners were being made to sing their death songs. Pierre shivered. He must save himself! They all seemed to be waiting for him to speak. Then he would!

"It was the Algonquin who wished to kill our people," he said.

His father and mother drew nearer.

"Tell us," encouraged his mother.

Pierre's heart leaped. Perhaps he would be able to save himself! He had not really wanted to kill the boys. His mother was looking eagerly down at him.

"I did not want our people killed," he told her.

She fell down on the floor in front of him, and tears rolled down her weathered cheeks.

"Oh, my son! My son, Orimha! It was all the fault of that wicked Algonquin. I knew it must be so!"

She turned to the chief.

"Save him! Save him!" she pleaded. "He is our son!"

But before the chief could reply, a group of warriors appeared in the doorway.

"We have come for the prisoner," they announced, and Pierre's heart sank. Once more, he summoned all his courage as they led him out to the spot where all the other prisoners were being tortured. He was pushed onto a scaffold with five men and three women. Then the melancholy chant, as they sang their death songs, together with the sickening odor of burning flesh made Pierre feel faint. If only he could run away from all this! But he knew any such attempt would be useless. Some of his former friends and acquaintances were pressing round the scaffold. Some struck him cruelly; some cut gashes in his flesh; others pressed his fingers into the bowls of lighted pipes and puffed away while Pierre gritted his teeth. The pain was almost beyond endurance, but he tried, with all the strength at his command, to keep from his set face any expression of the agony he was suffering. Sometimes, he could scarcely catch his breath, and sometimes he almost fainted.

Just how many hours these tortures continued, Pierre was not sure. But they suddenly ceased, for the sky became overcast and a great wind began to howl in the treetops. Lightning flashed, thunder rolled ominously; and great spatters of rain fell on all the assembled multitude. Most of the Indians ran for shelter, but a few were not to be denied their revenge.

Soon, however, the wind lashed with new fury, bending and swaying the treetops as if to break off even the toughest of them. As the rain came down in torrents, the prisoners, heads bowed to the storm, were left deserted, bound to their places on the scaffolds.

At first, Pierre was grateful for the interruption of the storm. But as the force of the wind buffeted him about, and poured rivulets of water into his many wounds, he felt that his pain-racked and shivering body could endure no more. Then, with a pounding roar, great hail stones descended in stinging blows on his naked and helpless body. Pierre closed his eyes and breathed a prayer.

That night he and the other prisoners were dragged from the scaffolds, and, still naked, tied to posts. Pierre shivered in the cold air that followed the storm. In the semi-darkness, three figures were coming toward him. Had he not suffered enough for one day? But his heart leaped as he saw

63

it was his mother and Conharraffen and A-we-not, bringing him food.

They said nothing as they fed him. Did they still care? And could they do anything to save him? He tried to speak; but they merely shook their heads at him and walked away. It was a long, long night for Pierre.

The second day, was, if anything, worse than the first. All day long, fresh wounds were inflicted on top of the previous day's unhealed sores. When, at last, nightfall came, and the prisoners were removed once more from their scaffolds and tied to their posts for the night, Pierre dared to hope there would be a respite. But just then, he saw advancing toward him a woman and a little boy. The boy carried a knife, and the woman forced him to attempt to cut off one of Pierre's fingers. The child's hands were not strong enough. He haggled at the flesh. Pierre could scarcely restrain a low moan. But he bit his tongue and endured all the pain until, at last, the woman made the little boy suck the wound. Then she pulled the child away. Pierre knew that the Indians believed this would make the boy brave.

On the third day, Pierre felt he could stand no more — and yet the tortures continued. There was scarcely an inch of his flesh which was not cut or burned; live coals and burning pipes had been pressed against his feet until they were so swollen and blistered he could hardly stand. By noon, his pain-racked body had reduced him to half-consciousness; and, as if in a dream, he realized his multilated form was being untied and dragged from the scaffold. Was this to be the end?

Across the village they continued to drag him, past many cabins, and into the Long House. There, still feeling as if he were in a trance, he beheld a circle of fifty or sixty old men smoking their pipes, and holding council. Pierre's swollen and bleeding feet would hardly support him, and his knees began to bend like hinges. The warriors who had pulled him into the council house left him alone. He must stand; for he knew this was to be his trial. What would they decide to do with him?

CHAPTER X

For some moments there was complete silence in the Long House. Then, Pierre's foster father and brother entered. Pierre looked at them, but they gave no sign that he meant anything to them. He felt a little heartened, however, when he saw they carried plenty of wampum. Perhaps they were going to plead for him, after all. Pierre knew that wampum, more precious to an Indian than money, was presented as a gift when making a petition before a council. He waited anxiously.

But he was not to know his fate so soon, for all the other captives were being brought in, too. And he stood, tense and suffering, while he heard them condemned to death or made slaves of the Indians. Then, at last, his turn came, and an Indian forced him to sit on the floor in the center of the council. Every inch of his body ached. Pierre looked toward his father. But his father was gazing straight ahead. Pierre saw he carried, besides many pieces of wampum, his medicine bag which was supposed to be so powerful as to contain the strength of the Sun, the Moon, and the Earth.

As his father stepped forward to speak, Pierre's burns and cuts were paining so that it seemed as if he would faint. This he must not let himself do! He watched his father as he advanced to the center of the circle and stood only a few feet from Pierre. His voice boomed out, filling the Long House to its very corners. In spite of his almost unbearable pain, Pierre noticed how loud were his father's tones; and Pierre knew the Indians would be impressed, for, the louder the speech, the better they liked it.

Warmed by the fire, Pierre's many cuts and bruises began to throb. He held his breath to keep from crying out, as shooting pains racked his entire body; and, all at once, he felt himself reeling. The whole room seemed to be rocking and swaying, and all the assembled Indians seemed to be reeling, also. Pierre straightened his shoulders and half closed his eyes. He must not become dizzy, and he must not

65

faint. He gritted his teeth and blinked hard. His father had already thrown one large piece of wampum; and his voice was growing louder and louder.

"This was my son, Orimha! He has done wrong; but he has suffered. He has endured tortures. He has proved he is a man!"

Then his father threw down another piece of wampum, and continued, in a still louder voice.

"If he, alone, had killed our people, he still must die!"

Pierre felt very faint again, but he strove to make himself listen to what his foster father was saying. He was shouting, now.

"But it was not my son who did this horrible deed. It was the Algonquin, Te-cum-seh. He made my son do as he said! He, and he alone is to blame!"

Pierre could feel himself swaying again. He was no longer sure of what his father was saying. He blinked his eyes and shook his head. He must not faint.

Then he saw his mother enter. And she danced and sang to please the council. He watched her throw down a large belt of wampum in the center of the council floor. And he watched while his brother, with a hatchet in his hand, sang a war song, and then departed. How much longer would this drag on? Next, Pierre realized that his father was standing up again, and he, also sang. Then, he, too, left, and Pierre was all alone with the council. He felt bereft of every friend. What would the council decide?

For a long time they debated. Why did they not get it over with? If they were going to kill him, why did they not do it quickly? He was in such pain by now that he no longer cared what happened.

After a time, there was a noise behind him. It was torture to look around; but, when he did, he was surprised to see that other Indians, many of them his former friends, were opening up the sides of the Long House; and crowds of them were standing there, staring at him. Were they just waiting to take him away from the council? There was a stir in the crowd, and Pierre saw his father entering once more. He stood again before the council, threw down more wampum, and once more sang and spoke.

Hopelessly, Pierre closed his eyes. If the council would not let him go before, why should they now? It was no use. He might as well be resigned to his fate. Never again would he see his own people. The crowds were waiting to kill him. He blinked back the hot tears. But just then someone grasped his arm. Someone was cutting the ropes which bound him! He opened his eyes. It was his foster father untying him and pulling him to his feet!

"Orimha! My son!" he was saying.

Then Pierre knew he was to be freed! He forgot his weakness, and the awful pain. He forgot his hopelessness! In spite of his burns and wounds, he mustered an almost superhuman strength and danced and sang for all the Indians. Because he was so suddenly relieved of his awful fear, he hardly noticed the pain of his blistered feet. He knew the Indians would be pleased if he danced. That, in fact, they would expect it of him.

What a shouting and singing there was, then! His father and mother, his two sisters and his brother entered and joined wholeheartedly in the dancing and singing. Louder and louder they sang and danced for joy at his release. But soon, they stopped, and, half carrying Pierre they took him to his former cabin home, while a great crowd followed and stood outside.

There, they laid him tenderly on the fur-covered boards which served as his bed. And his mother knelt beside him and held his hand.

"Orimha, my son! My son! You have suffered tortures like a true Indian. Now I will fix your wounds."

She bade Conharraffan and A-we-not to bring water, and Pierre all but fainted when she scraped his wounds with a knife. Then, having sprayed them with water from her mouth, she covered them with plaster made from some roots, which his father had collected, and which his sisters had prepared by chewing. Gradually, the pain began to lessen. Gratefully, Pierre closed his eyes and, exhausted as he was, he fell into a deep sleep.

CHAPTER XI

It was almost two weeks before Pierre's wounds were healed, and a month before he was able to touch his feet to the ground. But the weeks passed quickly, and Pierre settled down once more into the Indian way of living. Only his middle finger was lame. It was very comfortable to be waited on and fussed over by his mother and sisters; to have the companionship of his father, brother, and his friends. Everywhere he went, everyone showered him with gifts, and he came to look forward to each new moon, for it was then that his father presented him with a new white shirt with a wide Dutch collar. He knew the Indians could not have made these shirts, for they were of cloth which had been woven on a loom. Where did they come from? He approached his mother.

"My mother," he said, "these are beautiful shirts which my father gives me. They must come from far away."

His mother smiled, "Indeed, they do, my son. They are from the pale faces who live toward the rising sun. Our people go there to trade. Perhaps you can go some day, too, when we get enough furs."

These white people must be the Dutch at Fort Orange, he thought, for he had heard of this settlement when he was back at Three Rivers. How he wished he could see it, and see white people once more! Yet he knew he must not yet ask for any favors. He would have to watch his chance. Perhaps the opportunity might come.

At last, winter set in. Altho Pierre longed very often for his warm home back at Three Rivers, he was not uncomfortable in this Indian settlement. His mother and sisters waited on him; his brother took him trapping, and his father let him know, in many ways, that he was fond of him. On many days, after the snow came, he and his brother and Ya-le-wah-noh had great fun out of doors.

Sometimes, they sat on pieces of rawhide and slid down hill. Sometimes, they played snow snake. This game Pierre liked best of all. They would search until they found a straight, slender limb of a tree which had a gnarled piece like a head on one end. Stripping off the bark, they would rub and polish the stick until it shone like satin.

Then, he and the other young men of the village would drag a log back and forth in the snow to make a trough over which they poured water so that the sides would become walls of ice. Then, each in turn would hurl his stick, gnarled end foremost, down the trough. As it slithered against the rounded, icy sides, it looked not unlike a snake wriggling rapidly along. Often the boys would form teams of six each and vie with each other; for the ones who hurled their snow snakes furthest, won. It was great fun, and Pierre became so proficient that he could hurl his snow snake as far as any of the rest, and, once in a while, a little further. Many times they challenged teams from neighboring villages.

But not all the thoughts of these Indians, during the winter, were of play. More and more often, the warriors painted their faces, made great speeches, sang, and performed war dances.

One day, when Pierre and his brother were watching some of these dances, Pierre was amazed to see, rushing from several cabins, about twenty Indians, some wearing armor and helmets made of thin reeds braided together, and all armed with axes, clubs or sticks. They were shouting loudly as they ran, and, when the rest saw them, they, too, joined in with lusty clamorings.

Above the tumult Pierre at last made out that they were yelling,

"The savages are preparing and arming!"

In alarm, Pierre turned questioningly toward his brother. But Hoh-squa-sa-ga-deh only smiled and said,

"It is nothing. They are playing with one another."

By this time the Indians had formed into two teams, and they were fighting and throwing each other. Those who were protected by the armor and helmets had to dodge the blows of the axes and clubs.

The crowd cheered as they fought their mock battle. At length, they closed in on each other, dragging those who were downed by the hair, just as they would have done to their enemies before cutting off their scalps.

Every day, there were demonstrations and preparations for war. Once more, Pierre approached his brother.

"Where do they go to fight?" he asked.

"To the Algonquins and French along the Great River." was the reply.

Pierre's heart leaped into his throat at these words. They were going to fight his own people! Troubled and unhappy, he walked away. What should he do? If he was to be respected and held in esteem by the Indians, he knew he must go on the warpath. Now that he had withstood torture, he would be expected to prove he was a great warrior, fitting son of a brave chief. How could he go on this expedition? He would be expected to fight and kill his own French people, or else the Algonquin Indians who had always been friendly to the French. This was terrible! Whatever would he do? What could he do?

One day, while he was turning all this over in his mind, he heard some of the young warriors talking.

"While they are fighting the French and Algonquins," they were saying, "we could make war on our enemies to the west. That is a land rich with beaver. Let us kill our enemies there, and get many beaver skins."

Pierre joined the group and listened eagerly to the rest of the discussion. This might be the solution of his problem! He was relieved when, as they finished their discussion, they turned to him,

"You would like to come, too, Orimha?" they asked.

Pierre was greatly excited at the thought. For a long time he had been growing weary of doing nothing much all day long. This would mean some action; and it would serve the double purpose of avoiding a war with his own people, and of giving him a chance of getting some beaver skins. This would be wonderful!

But he concealed his eagerness. He did not want them to guess how anxious he was to go with them.

"I will ask my mother and father," he replied.

They were both in the cabin when he reached it. Trying to appear casual, he stood quietly before them and addressed them.

"My father and mother," he began. "Many brave young Mohawks go toward the setting sun to make war on our enemies, and to get beaver skins. I am a Mohawk. I have proved that I am a warrior, also. And I wish to get many beaver skins. I would go with them."

His mother and father said nothing. Did they suspect his motives? He turned pleadingly toward his father. "You go with many brave men to make war on the enemies of the Mohawk. Let me prove that I, too, am a Mohawk of valor, and a true warrior. I would go with my Mohawk friends. I would help fight our enemies toward the setting sun."

Pierre's father looked at him for a moment. Pierre held his breath and clenched his finger nails into the palms of his hands. Then, after what seemed an hour, "It is good," his father said. "You may go."

Pierre was overjoyed that all his present problems were taken care of. He hurried back to tell the rest he had permission to make war with them.

The next few days were spent in preparation. His mother packed a basket with food and provided a kettle for cooking; his sisters made ready his clothing; and his father and brother helped him in making ready his weapons. At last the day of departure arrived, and he and his friends set out.

For some time, Pierre and his companions traveled west, through friendly Iroquois country where they were well received. But at length, enemy country was reached. It was a bloody business, this stalking, attacking, and killing. And Pierre did not relish it much. But, if he must kill, it was better to attack strangers. Anything was better than having to fight his own people!

71

Many weeks later, he and his party started back home. The rest were full of glee over all the enemies they had killed, the prisoners they had taken, and the many beaver skins they had stolen from their enemies. But Pierre felt a little sick as he thought of what they had done.

When, at last, they reached their own village, and word of their return spread through the settlement, excited villagers crowded round them, shouting their welcome, and forming into two long lines ready for the prisoners who would be made to run the gauntlet. Pierre wished he could do something to stop the tortures which he knew would follow; but he was powerless.

Just then, he saw his mother and sisters running toward him; and grabbing up his share of the furs, he hurried to greet them. His mother grasped his arm; his sisters crowded round.

"Orimha!" they exclaimed together. "You are safe!"

They led him into their cabin and seated him in the place of honor.

"You are truly a warrior!" his mother exclaimed proudly as she brought him food and bade his sisters comb his hair. Pierre was glad to be back. It was comforting to be cared for once more.

"We have many beaver skins," he announced.

"That is good," said his mother. "We can trade them with the pale faces toward the rising sun."

The pale faces toward the rising sun! How he longed to see white men once more! This would be wonderful! How soon would they go, and would they allow him to make the trip, too? But, not daring to show undue eagerness, he crowded back his feelings, continued eating, and said nothing.

The days went by, pleasantly enough. Sometimes, he and other young men played lacrosse. They would drive two posts several feet apart into the ground. Then, about five hundred feet from these posts they fastened in two others in a similar manner. Next, getting out their lacrosse sticks, and choosing sides, they played with a ball made of wood, or of stuffed buckskin. It was very exciting to try to get the ball between the other team's posts, and to strive to keep the other team from reaching their posts. The ball could be carried in the sticks, or thrown, but never touched with the hands.

Sometimes they played another game on the leveled ground outside the palisade. While some rolled wooden hoops, others attempted to hit them with spears. It was very difficult to strike a moving target, and at first Pierre's companions were greatly amused at his unsuccessful efforts, but after some practice, he also, became quite skilled.

The days and weeks passed, and still Pierre heard nothing more about any journey to the Dutch settlement. Was he to be cheated out of seeing white men again? Had they changed their minds, or were they waiting for the return of his foster father and the warriors who had gone to the north country? The fall season was beginning. He hoped they would not wait until winter for the journey.

One day, when his mother was grinding corn, he sat down beside her.

"My father has not yet come home," he stated, and waited to see what his mother might say.

She continued her work for a few moments. Then, calmly, she announced, "He will come, Orimah. You must not fear. He is a great chief, and a mighty warrior."

Again Pierre waited; but she said nothing more. All he could do, then, was to watch for anything which looked like preparations for a trading party.

Some weeks later, his patience was rewarded when one morning he saw his mother and sisters piling up furs in one corner of the cabin. He stood, watching, until his mother, glancing up, said, "Our people go soon toward the rising sun to trade furs with the pale faces. We have many skins. We will get much."

Pierre was overjoyed. Once more he would see white men. How very long it had been! Then, fear clutched at his heart. Would they let him go; or would they think he might

73

try to escape? He must know! Attempting to keep his voice steady, he asked, "Do I go too, my mother?"

"You go, too," she replied, and went on with her work.

Pierre was so overjoyed that he felt like helping her gather together the animal skins to speed preparations. But he knew he must not, for it would be beneath the dignity of a young warrior to work. Instead, he went over to his bunk and began looking over his possessions to see what he should wear for the journey.

Meanwhile, preparations continued in his and in several other cabins. The best skins were chosen and piled up, ready for the start. The women and girls of the village prepared food, and kettles in which to cook it.

The day of departure arrived; and, a small party having been chosen, they set out with about two hundred beaver skins. Pierre was very happy as they followed the trail to the east — happy because his Indian family trusted him, and happy that he was to see the white people once more. As he and Ya-le-wah-noh walked along with the rest, they sang; Ya-le-wah-noh encouraging Pierre to sing some French songs.

CHAPTER XII

For some days they followed the trail to the east along a river, pausing to be welcomed at several Mohawk villages along the way. One or two of these villages were small ones of but ten or twelve cabins huddled in the woods, while another larger one was protected by a single stockade. And one village of some twenty-four bark houses was perched on the edge of a hill about a bow shot from the river, and it was protected by a double stockade having four entrances.

Between villages, Pierre and his companions cared for themselves, stopping, whenever they were hungry, to eat food prepared by the squaws. At night, rolled in blankets, or animal skins, they slept on the bare ground with stones or bits of wood for pillows, their only shelter being the dense forest.

On the morning of the fourth day, Ya-le-wah-noh said to Pierre,

"We are almost at the cabins of the pale faces. Today we send messengers with the most beautiful skins."

Even as he spoke, some of the older men were selecting a few of the best pelts and giving them to two young men. Ya-le-wah-noh continued to talk as they were eating.

"When the pale faces see such beautiful skins, they will gather to trade."

He chewed on a piece of bear's meat which he held to his mouth with both hands.

"You will see. They will be glad to have our furs; and they will give us muskets and knives and shirts."

By this time, the messengers were off. Pierre was very impatient for their return, for, now that he was so close to a white man's settlement, he could hardly wait to get there. He counted up the time it had been since he had seen a white man. Almost a year and a quarter! A year and a quarter of seeing only painted and often dirty savages.

What would these people be like? They would not be his beloved French, but would be mostly Dutch; and he could not speak their language! However, just seeing white people again would make him happy. How very long it had been! Would any of these Dutch notice that he was not an Indian? And, if they did, would the Indians think he was trying to escape? Also, if they did believe this, would they torture him again? Mingled feelings of joy and fear made his heart beat faster.

Pierre glanced down at his buckskin trousers and moccasined feet. His bare torso and his hands and arms were tanned and weathered from his outdoor life. He knew his face must be equally browned, and, painted and dirty as it was, it must look similar to the faces of his companions. His brown hair cut in crested form and, like the others' smeared with bear's grease, should appear much darker than its natural color. Only his blue eyes could not be disguised. He would have to be careful to keep his eyes downcast so they would not be noticed. Then, if he kept with the Indians, the Dutch people might not discover him to be a white man.

Pierre's heart was pounding with excited anticipation, but he tried to appear calm as he stretched himself full length on the bare ground beside Ya-le-wah-Noh to wait. And, although it seemed an age to Pierre, it was, in reality, not long until the messengers were returning and exclaiming,

"The pale faces like our furs. They say come with all haste."

At once, every Indian was ready and eager to be off. With the men in the lead, and the women carrying the burdens, they started along the trail. They laughed and sang as they followed each other through the woods. Around each bend in the trail, Pierre strained his eyes to search out a clearing which would mean they were at the Dutch settlement. He could hardly wait! And then, at last, the trees suddenly thinned out in the sandy soil, and there, seeming to Pierre to be almost unreal, Fort Orange, with its twenty-five or thirty thatched-roofed houses, lay immediately below them.

At the foot of the hill, beyond the wooden-sided houses, the church and the fort, lay a great river sparkling in the morning sunshine. Its brilliant blue contrasted sharply with the autumn-hued foliage which was interspersed with spots of dark and stately evergreens lining each bank.

But Pierre had no time for further gazing, for, hurrying toward them from the settlement was a group of white men and boys, shouting greetings.

At the sight of these people, Pierre's emotions almost choked him. Eagerly, he drank in every detail of the men's appearance, — their clean, white hands, and pink-cheeked faces; — their European-like clothing consisting of leather, canvas, or homespun doublets, white shirts, breeches, hand-knitted stockings and leather shoes. Some wore knitted caps over their short, fair hair; some medium-brimmed felt hats, while others were bareheaded. A few had their sleeves rolled up and their shirts open at the throat; some had knives thrust through their leather belts. And all of them, men and boys alike, greeted the Indians joyfully and marched back with them into the settlement.

Here were more sights for Pierre's hungry eyes. Women and girls, in brightly-hued and kerchief-topped dresses, stood framed in doorways of the houses, watching the Indians. As they were passing down the street, a few women ventured outside and, with arms folded across the snowy white of their aprons, they stood staring at the visitors. One of the rosy-cheeked women made Pierre think of his own mother. How was she, he wondered? Hot tears stung his eyelids as he tried to blink them away.

The Indians were quiet in the company of the white men. There was no more singing or talking. Only the white men chattered together and bustled about collecting muskets, knives, and other articles in preparation for trading with their visitors.

Taking care to keep in the center of the Indian group, Pierre walked quietly with them. The white people were leading the way past the church and the fort, to a fair-sized building; and, clustered about the doorway was a group of boys who shouted excitedly when they caught sight of the procession. Although Pierre could not understand what they were saying, he knew they must be announcing the arrival of the Indians, for men appeared in the doorway and then retreated to allow the Indians to enter.

Inside the building, Pierre continued to keep well toward the center of the group of Indians clustered together at one end of the room. How he longed to rush over to the white men almost filling the rest of the room! To touch them! To shout, "I, too, am white!"

But fear kept Pierre rooted to his place, and he choked down his feelings and watched with half-closed eyes. Here were several white men in richer dress — one with silk doublet, touches of snowy white at the neck and wrists, and wearing a broad-brimmed, plumed hat. As he took up his position in front of a long crude table, swept off his hat and bowed, the room became suddenly quiet. The white men leaned against the wide boards of the walls, or took half-standing positions against other tables, or crowded on benches. The well-dressed man motioned to another to step forward, and, this one, speaking in the Mohawk tongue said,

"The white people greet our red brothers. For a long time, we have looked toward the setting sun to see if they come to visit us, their white brothers. Now they are here, and we welcome them."

From the group of Indians, one of the older warriors stepped forward. His skin was weathered and wrinkled from years of exposure; but his step was firm, and he held himself erectly. With great dignity, he folded his arms across his chest, and began to speak, first in low tones and then as his thoughts gathered momentum, in louder and louder tones, until the very rafters re-echoed the sounds.

"We, your red brothers, have come to our white brothers who dwell on the hill by the big river. Our squaws have carried our burdens, and the way was good. No demons who dwell in these forests brought harm to us! No trees, laden

78

with years, and that will soon be cast down to the earth by old age, delayed our progress. The Great Spirit was with us!"

"Now, we have come. We bring many beautiful furs. Our brave hunters have gathered these furs. No others could be better. We, the mighty Mohawks, have brought them to our white brothers. We wish muskets, and powder, and shirts. We, the Mohawks, have spoken!"

Then, the white man who understood the language stepped forward.

"We, your white brothers, have seen the furs which your messengers carried to us. They are indeed good. Have your squaws open your bundles. We, your white brothers are ready to trade."

At a sign from the Indian warrior, the squaws advanced to the tables, placed on them the great bundles of furs, and began to open them. At the sight bedlam broke loose; for no formal speeches could keep the white people from an immediate beginning of the trading. The Indians rushed to aid the squaws; the white people, laden with all they had brought for trading, pressed forward.

Ya-le-wah-noh grasped Pierre by the arm and hurried him to the milling group. He was pushed, elbowed, and jostled. Voices shouted in his ear. Even in the confusion he realized that some of these voices were English as well as Dutch. Furs and muskets were rapidly changing hands. Those white people who could not speak any Mohawk were resorting to sign language. Both Indians and white people were counting off on their fingers the number of skins offered or accepted for the white man's wares. Ya-le-wah-noh thrust some beaver skins into Pierre's arms.

"You trade!" he said, and turned toward a prospective customer of his own.

Pierre looked down at the beaver skins. They were especially choice ones; but he had no desire to trade. All he wanted to do was to stay in the background and drink his fill of the sight and sound of white people once more. But there was no time. For, no sooner did he find himself holding these furs than he was surrounded by several white men who wanted them, and they clutched at the furs and grasped Pierre's arm to get immediate attention.

Then, suddenly, someone was grabbing Pierre by the shoulders, turning him around so violently that the beaver skins went flying in all directions. And he found himself staring into the astonished eyes of a dark-haired man.

"Mon Dieu!" the man was exclaiming.

Startled at the French words, Pierre could only stand, frozen in the man's grasp.

"Mon Dieu!" he was exclaiming again. "You're no painted Indian!"

When Pierre still said nothing, the man shook him.

"Are you?" he persevered, the words pouring out in rapid French. "You can't be! You have blue eyes, and your hair isn't black. You look French."

He shook Pierre again, and, thrusting his face into Pierre's.

"Are you French?" he demanded.

Pierre could be still no longer; and, at his whispered, "Oui," the Frenchman embraced him and pulled him across the room and outside the building.

"I knew it! I knew it!" he kept exclaiming.

He backed Pierre up against the side of the building and flung questions at him.

"Who are you, lad? And how did you get here in all this Indian disguise? Where is your home?"

By now, Pierre's surprise at hearing his native tongue had given way to fear of being noticed by the Indians.

"Sh!" he cautioned. "They may hear us!"

Nodding his understanding, the Frenchman led Pierre past several houses and into the shelter of a cluster of bushes. There, he renewed his bombardment of questions; and Pierre could hardly keep back tears of relief as he poured out his story. Every now and then, the Frenchman exclaimed in sympathy at the details. He examined the scars which testified to Pierre's tortures, and almost wept over them. Every time Pierre paused for breath, the Frenchman plied him with more questions.

But at last Pierre's story was done, and the Frenchman pulled Pierre to him.

"You poor boy!" he kept exclaiming. "You poor boy!" Then he slapped Pierre on the back.

"But that is all over now! Come! Let us go see the governor! I, Jacques Dieppe, will take you to him. He will help you!"

And Jacques led Pierre arm in arm out from the sheltering bushes and down the street. Pierre was too overcome with emotion to protest. Would the Indians see them? Glancing fearfully about him, he took heart at seeing none of them. It must be they were still trading.

There were a few white people about, and Jacques called to them in Dutch. Although Pierre could not understand, he needed no interpreter to know that Jacques was telling them that he had another Frenchman with him.

People stopped to stare; they hurried up to Pierre to gaze intently at him. Some ran to tell others. A crowd soon gathered about Pierre and Jacques, and excitement mounted. Women urged them into their homes for food and drink. Men and boys followed, pulling on Pierre's arms, jostling their neighbors for a closer view — chattering intently.

Within a few minutes, the crowd had reached a house larger than its neighbors, and, after some of the men had knocked and pounded on the door with their bare fists, Pierre found himself half pushed, and half carried inside.

As if in a dream, he beheld once more white people's furniture — tables, chairs, benches. How strange it seemed after all these months! Even the milling crowd could not entirely blot out fleeting glimpses of these objects of civilization. From somewhere, one man's voice rose above the tumult of the crowded room. His tones were those of one in authority. The crowds fell back, the tumult ceased. Pierre was pushed forward and found himself facing a sturdy, fair-haired Dutchman whose kindly-blue eyes belied the firm set of his jaw.

81

His sleeveless doublet of fine, blue silk, his breeches of some dark woolen material, his light, blue shirt, his snowy-white-linen collar all bespoke the gentleman. Standing there, with Jacques holding him firmly by the arm, Pierre trembled with excitement.

Afterward, Pierre was never very clear as to everything which occurred in the next few minutes. To his surprise, the Dutch governor spoke in French and Jacques spoke to the crowd sometimes in French, sometimes in Dutch. Then, prompted by Jacques, Pierre was again telling his story, while those who understood, exclaimed in sympathy, and those who did not, strove to find someone who could translate for them.

At the conclusion, Jacques and the governor drew to one side of the room and engaged in an animated conversation. From the tones, Pierre could tell that there were questions and answers; and occasional suggestions from the crowd. At length, Jacques turned to Pierre and spoke in his native tongue.

"It is all arranged, my Pierre! You will stay here with us; for the governor, himself, will arrange for your ransom."

Jacques threw one arm across Pierre's shoulder.

"My friend, Pierre, how happy I am! Are you, too, happy? Once more you will live with white people! Once more you will eat white men's food! We will take off this paint; we will give you clean clothes. You will be happy here!"

At these words, Pierre felt a cold despair settling over him. With every fiber of his being, he longed to do the very things of which Jacques had spoken. But how could he? How would the Indians receive this offer? The memory of all the tortures he had suffered after his last attempt to escape, filled him with terror. He could never endure that again.

Seeing his hesitation, there spread over Jacques face a look of alarm. He pressed closer to Pierre.

"What do you say?" he demanded anxiously. "Did you not understand? We will ransom you from these dirty Indians!"

Pierre drew in a frightened breath.

"No! No!" he exclaimed. "You must not do that! It might make the Indians very angry, for I am a chief's son; and I do not believe they would allow me to be taken from them."

Jacques protested loudly. He called on the governor, and upon the assembled crowd to persuade Pierre to agree. Great confusion broke out. Everyone talked at once. Those who had not found room inside were craning their necks and questioning their neighbors to learn what was the trouble. Jacques was insistent.

"You cannot say this!" he cried. "You must stay here! How can you ever go back with these Indians? You are young and have many years of life ahead of you. Do you intend to spend all the rest of your days away from your own people?"

The governor spoke pleadingly, "You must let us do this thing for you."

Dry sobs shook Pierre so he could hardly speak, but he managed to blurt out.

"No! It cannot be! Thank you; but I would not dare! I have to go back!"

Sobbing to himself, he pushed blindly through the crowd and out onto the street, with Jacques close at his heels. All the way back to the building where the Indians were trading, Jacques kept pleading with him, and the crowd followed excitedly.

Inside the building, the fur trading was still going on. Pierre hurried over to the Indians and tried to lose himself among them. But Jacques remained beside him, and Ya-le-wah-noh looked questionly at them.

"Please," whispered Pierre under his breath. "Do not let them know!"

Jacques pressed Pierre's arm, and, nodding reassuringly, whispered, "I will see you again." He sauntered off into the crowd. Pierre kept a little distance from Ya-le-wah-noh. It might be that he would forget Pierre's recent absence if he did not stay near him.

The fur trading continued briskly, and it was not until sunset time that the supplies were exhausted. Then the

Indians, laden with their booty went outside, and, squatting on the ground or leaning up against the sides of the building, ate the food which the squaws prepared. Clustered here and there, white men and boys stood, watching. As Pierre attempted to eat, he saw Jacques coming toward him, but he dared not appear to recognize him, for Ya-le-wah-noh was not far off.

Jacques stood in front of him; but Pierre did not look up. Jacques dropped down beside him and spoke in low tones,

"Why do you not come with me tonight, my Pierre? My cabin is not large, but you would like it. You could sleep once again in a white man's bed. You could eat once more white man's food. Will you not come just for tonight?"

Pierre swallowed hard, and set his jaw.

"I dare not!" he whispered. "Please, for my sake, do not talk to me anymore today," he pleaded.

Jacques rose, slowly.

"Very well, my Pierre, but I will see you in the morning." And he was gone.

Ya-le-wah-noh wandered over and sat down beside Pierre.

"Is white man your friend?" he asked bluntly.

Pierre roused himself from his thoughts.

"I never saw him before today," he answered.

Apparently satisfied, Ya-le-wah-noh asked no more, but he remained near Pierre. When darkness fell, the Indians rolled themselves in their blankets, some sleeping in the shelter of the Dutchmen's barns, some on the floor of the building where they had done their trading. For a long time, Pierre did not close his eyes, and then slept, fitfully, as he miserably turned the day's happenings over and over in his thoughts.

Early the next morning, the Indians were up, making ready for the return journey. It was a heavy-hearted Pierre who sat with them and pretended to eat. Here was his long-hoped-for chance to escape; and he dared not take it! The Indians were ready to set out now. What about Jacques? Would he ever see him again? Even as he was thinking of him, the Frenchman came in sight, hurrying to Pierre's side.

Throwing his arms around Pierre, he pleaded with him, as he had the day before.

"My friend, Pierre," he entreated. "For the last time, I beg of you to stay. Come with me, once more to the Governor. He will arrange for your ransom!"

Pierre was even more frightened than he had been the previous day, for, even though the Indians could not understand Jacques' words, Ya-le-wah-noh was scowling at him, and the other Indians were staring, their faces impassive.

Pierre hardened his expression, and gazed straight ahead as he answered.

"Please, Jacques," he begged. "Do you not see how they all stare? Even though they say nothing, I know they are becoming angry. If you do not go back, there will be trouble."

Pierre's voice shook.

"With all my heart, I would like to stay, but I dare not. They might kill you, and they would torture, perhaps even kill me this time. Please, Jacques, for my sake." He was speaking rapidly now. "Perhaps I can think of some way, but not now. Please, please, go back!"

With tears streaming down his face, Jacques embraced Pierre.

"Goodby, my friend," he murmured. "May God bless you, and bring you back some day!" And he was gone.

The Indian women began to pick up their burdens, and the whole company started to file out of the settlement, past the wooden houses; past the few white people gathered to witness their departure. For a short time, they marched in silence. Then, when they were once again on the wooden trail, Ya-le-wah-noh fell into step beside Pierre.

"The white man want you to stay?" he inquired shrewdly.

Pierre, still too filled with emotion to speak, merely nodded his head. Then, fearful he had done the wrong thing, he hastily summoned his courage, and, with a great effort, managed to say, "I tell him I am Mohawk."

"Yes," agreed Ya-le-wah-noh, "You are Mohawk." And he walked quietly and thoughtfully beside Pierre.

After they had marched through the woods for some time, had rested and eaten, and then started off once more, the Indians appeared to have forgotten the incident. They sang and rejoiced over all the booty they had obtained from the white men; and, to offset their suspicions, Pierre tried to join in with the singing and laughing. But never once in the days they were on the trail, did the heavy feeling of bitter disappointment leave his aching heart.

When on the fourth day, the familiar Indian village came into view, and they filed inside the stockade, past the rejoicing and welcoming Indians, he felt as if the enclosing walls were shutting him in forever.

CHAPTER XIII

For several days, Pierre brooded over what he had done. Had he made a foolish mistake? Should he have let the Dutch ransom him? Since he had not seized that opportunity, when would he get another chance? Sometime, of course, the Indians might go hunting near the St. Lawrence River. If they let him go with them, he might steal away to Three Rivers. But how could he, without their guessing his purpose? **And if he were not near his old house, how could he be sure he** would ever find his way? On the other hand, since he had been with white people again, how could he stand it to live for an unknown length of time with these savages? To be sure, they had made him one of them; they had been good to him when he had submitted to them. But would it last? His Indian father was even now still fighting the French people — Pierre's own people. What had happened back up north in his old home?

At length, Pierre approached his Indian mother.

"My mother," he began. "My brave father has been away a long time. I am fearful that the fighting may have been great. Is it not time for him and his braves to be back?"

His foster mother paused in her work.

"Your father is truly a brave and valiant fighter. There is none better. He will be back."

But Pierre noticed a flicker of anxiety cross her face as if she were saying this last statement out loud to convince herself, even more than him.

At the end of another week, when there was still no news of his Indian father, Pierre became greatly worried. What if his own French people had killed him? Would the Indians exact vengeance on him, because he was a Frenchman? Pierre shuddered at the thought.

When day after day had passed, with still no word, Pierre grew almost desperate. Had he made a mistake not to listen to Jacques' pleading? All one night through, he slept scarcely at all for puzzling over what to do. When the first pale rays of the autumn sun began to dispel the chill of dawn, Pierre had made his decision.

"I will go back to Fort Orange," he told himself, "for, if my Indian father has been killed, these Mohawks will probably kill me for revenge. If I plan carefully, perhaps I can reach the Dutch, and my friend Jacques. They will protect me; they will help me. But this time, I will go alone. If I tell everyone I am going hunting, they will not miss me for at least a whole day. That will give me enough of a start so that I may be able to get there safely without being caught."

Pierre realized, fully, the great risk he was running; but, for the first time in days, he felt light-hearted and free.

During the morning, Pierre waited until some young Indians were about the village where they would see him. Then he went into the edge of the woods to cut sticks. When he returned, his brother was in the cabin. Throwing down his sticks, he said to him,

"How would you like to go hunting?"

Pierre smiled to himself, because he was certain his brother would say no. For Pierre knew his brother was tired from having just returned from the war path. Also, there was a pretty young Indian girl whom his brother liked, and Pierre was sure he would not wish to leave her again so soon. Therefore, he was not surprised when his brother said, absently,

"Maybe some other time. Not now."

Pierre was pleased. Now, when he had left, his brother would believe he had really gone hunting. He would cut more sticks, and let more Indians see him prepare for a hunting trip. For several days, he continued this ruse. Then, one night he said to himself.

"Tomorrow, I will start. And I will fool them further by leaving all my fine clothes and my presents in the cabin. Because I often wear some of them, they will not believe I have gone away without them."

Early the next morning Pierre awaited his chance. When there were no Indians looking, he strolled towards the woods, and, once out of sight, he started to run. Since he was dressed lightly, and carried only a hatchet and a knife, he could travel quickly.

"I must not follow the trail," he thought. "For, if any of them follow me, and find me there, they will know I am trying to escape to the Dutch settlement. But if I keep north of the trail, and they overtake me, I can simply say I got lost in the woods. How could they prove anything different?"

All that day, and all night, Pierre ran through the woods. He was glad, now, that he had gone on the warpath with the young Indians last winter. It had hardened him, and taught him how to make his way. But even so, after several hours had gone by, he began to feel tired. To keep from thinking of his weariness, he forced himself to cling desperately to his hope of reaching Fort Orange. He thought of Jacques; of how interested the Dutch people had been in his plight; of the kindness of the Dutch governor.

Then, he thought of the Mohawks whom he had left.

"I must hurry!" he kept telling himself, "or they may catch me." He shuddered. "That must not happen again."

On and on, he forced his weary legs, stopping only occasionally at some small stream for a hasty drink, finding his way as best he could through another night.

At last, in the early morning, he saw a small clearing in the woods; and, stealthily he crept from tree to tree until he could make out a small cabin. In front of it was a Dutchman chopping wood. Was he all alone, Pierre wondered? He dared not walk out boldly into the clearing; for there might be some Indians somewhere who might see him. Quietly, he crept close to the edge of the clearing and called softly to the man. At first, the man did not hear him. But, when he did, he came as Pierre motioned to him.

"I cannot tell him everything," thought Pierre, "but I must have his help."

He spoke in the Indian tongue.

"You want nice furs?" he asked the Dutchman.

Pierre was relieved when the Dutchman, looking pleased, answered in the Mohawk tongue.

"Yes," he answered, "of course. Let me see them."

Pierre put his finger to his mouth and looked about. "Is anyone else here?" he asked.

"Just my wife."

Pierre whispered, "Then I talk to you inside."

The Dutchman, still carrying his axe, led Pierre into his cabin where a woman was cooking breakfast, and a large dog was sleeping beside the fire. The food smelled so good Pierre felt faint, for he had not eaten since leaving the Mohawk village.

"You give me food?" he asked.

The Dutchman motioned to Pierre to sit down, and then, turning to his wife, he said, "Give him something to eat. He has some furs to trade."

Pierre ate greedily, smacking his lips as the savages did, and using his fingers, Indian fashion. When he finished eating, the Dutchman said, "Now, let us look at your furs."

But Pierre shook his head. "No, not yet. I have a message for the governor at Fort Orange. How far is it?"

"Two miles," replied his host. Pierre felt breathless to think he was so close to possible freedom. "You could get a message to the Governor?" he inquired.

"Of course," replied the puzzled Dutchman.

"Then give me something. I write."

The Dutchman stared, open mouthed at Pierre.

"You an Indian, can write!" he exclaimed.

Pierre lowered his tell-tale blue eyes. He was quick with his answer. "I have been a long time with the French; and they taught me to read and write a little."

Still with a wondering look on his face, the Dutchman produced paper, ink, and a quill pen. Quickly, Pierre wrote.

"Greetings to his Excellency, the Governor. You will remember me as the Frenchman who came to Fort Orange with the Mohawk Indians. I have escaped from them to within two miles of Fort Orange. But I dare not venture further without help for fear of prowling Mohawks who might be in this vicinity. Could you send a few men to escort me?

Your obedient servant,
Pierre Esprit Radisson"

The awed Dutchman and his wife were still staring at Pierre as he folded the note. Since it was in French, he hoped this man could not read it. For, thought Pierre to himself, it is much safer for me, just now, to make him think I am an Indian with valuable furs. He will be more likely to protect me until help comes. He held out the note.

"You will take this to the Governor?"

"Yes! Yes! But what about the furs?"

"First, this message must be taken. The furs are hidden in the woods for fear other Indians might steal them. It will take two days to reach them, but we can get them when you come back. They are very fine furs. Can you hurry?"

"Yes, indeed!" responded the Dutchman, and grabbing his coat, he was out the door. Pierre sighed with relief. He had been afraid this man would not leave his wife alone with someone he thought to be a savage.

Now that his message was really on its way to the governor, Pierre could take time to look about the tidy cabin, and the neat woman working beside the fireplace. He smiled to himself as he noticed that she kept close to the now growling dog which she was making only very feeble attempts to pacify. What would she think, Pierre wondered, when she learned how truly harmless he was, and that he was as white as she?

But these thoughts did not amuse him for long, for he was still apprehensive about any prowling Indians. Perhaps he could persuade the Dutch woman to hide him. He turned to her.

"Do not be afraid of me," he said. "See, I throw down my weapons," and he laid his knife and axe on the floor. "If other Indians find I am here," he continued, "they will make me tell where I am keeping my furs. Could you hide me until your husband comes back? I have beautiful furs," he reminded her. With his foot, Pierre pushed the knife and axe away from him.

The woman regarded him for a moment. "Yes, indeed," she replied. "Over there!" And she pointed to some sacks of wheat. By rearranging them, Pierre made a place to crawl under. Then the woman gave him a blanket to sit on, and put a sack over the space where he had crawled in. Pierre was cramped and hot in his hiding place. But he did not care, if only he could be safe until help arrived.

Night came, and still the Dutchman had not returned. Had something happened to him? It was very quiet in the cabin, for the Dutchman's wife had gone to bed. Pierre strained his ears for some sound which would mean her husband was returning, but the only sound of human beings he heard all night long, were some Indians singing as they went by. Pierre shuddered until they were gone. And once in a while, when there was only the whisper of the wind in the tree tops, he dozed for a brief space of time.

At last, dawn came. Soon the Dutchwoman was up making a fire and getting breakfast. She urged Pierre to come out of his hiding place; but he was afraid. It would be too bad to spoil everything by one false move.

"No," he replied. "I will remain hidden until your husband comes."

Just when it seemed as if his cramped muscles could stand the strain no longer, he heard footsteps. Peeking out, he saw the Dutchman and several other men. One of them looked like Jacques, and he moved to get a better view. It was Jacques! Pierre could contain his feeling no longer. With a cry of joy, he crawled forth from his hiding place, and, running past the startled Dutch woman, he threw his arms around Jacques' neck. Jacques embraced Pierre, and, rocking back and forth before their astonished audience, they exclaimed together in French.

The Dutchmen crowded around them, and at last succeeded in pulling them apart. All were asking questions at the same time, so Jacques had to translate for Pierre.

"How did you get here?"

"Did any Indians follow you?"

"Did you come alone?"

Jacques put up his hand for silence.

"Let us get this young man safely inside the fortress. Then he can answer all our questions."

He turned to Pierre. "We brought some clothing to disguise you." Then, to the still gaping Dutchwoman, "Some water, quickly," he ordered.

For a moment longer, she stared at Pierre, but, at Jacques' second demand for water, she moved fast enough to do his bidding. However, she continued to stare as Pierre washed his face, and the real color of his skin became evident. He could not help laughing as he saw the expression on her face, and heard her husband's startled exclamation. Pierre spoke to them in the Mohawk tongue.

"I really am not an Indian. The Mohawks captured me and made me one of them." Then he faced her husband. "I am sorry about the furs; but, because I knew nothing about you, I was afraid you might not help me unless you believed I could reward you. I am sorry."

The Dutchman and his wife grasped Pierre's hands. There were tears in the woman's eyes. "That is all right," they murmured.

But Jacques interrupted. "Hurry!" he said. "The Governor said to make all possible haste. It is too bad about the furs, young man; but we must be off where you can be protected before any Mohawk Indians come for you."

So they thanked the Dutchman and his wife, and set off, walking briskly along the trail to Fort Orange. As they entered the settlement, Pierre began to feel as if this was all a dream. All the settlement, it seemed, was there to greet him. Some shouted and cheered; children called out to him, dogs barked; everyone stared as if at some great curiosity. Pierre waved and smiled back. It was wonderful to see only white people again; to be walking past white man's cabins; to see clean faces, and clean hands, and clean clothes.

When they reached the Governor's house, Pierre was warmly greeted and bidden to sit down.

The Governor smiled kindly as he spoke, "We welcome you, my friend. We cannot tell you how happy we are to know that you are safely back here with us."

93

Pierre attempted to express his gratitude, but Jacques interrupted.

"I must tell the governor what danger you are still in. I, Jacques, know these Indians, my Pierre. Because you are a chief's son, they will leave no stone unturned to find you. We must hide you until we can decide how best to help you. And we must hurry to warn everyone to keep silent about your having come. No Indians must be told a thing! We must post watches for any Mohawks, so we can be warned."

Jacques spoke rapidly to the governor who nodded his assent, and delivered quick orders to several of the Dutchmen in the room. Then Pierre was whisked out of the governor's house and down the street to Jacques' small cabin. Behind them, the Dutchmen were scurrying to spread the governor's warning.

For two days, Pierre kept hidden in Jacques' cabin. He had no chance to be lonesome, for almost everyone at Fort Orange came to see him. They gave him clothes; they brought him food. Those who could speak the Indian tongue plied him with questions; those who could not, asked Jacques to interpret for them.

How good it seemed to Pierre to be with white people again; to wear white people's clothes; to feel clean! And how he and the others laughed when it took repeated washings to get all the bears' grease from his hair. They made great sport of his strange, crested haircut, even as they attempted to do what they could to improve it. For the first time since Pierre had been taken prisoner, he felt really happy.

CHAPTER XIV

On the third morning after Pierre's arrival, Jacques stepped from the cabin to get a pail of water. But the door had scarcely closed behind him when he rushed breathlessly back.

Pierre!" he exclaimed. "You must hide! Over here! The sentries have just warned that a party of Mohawks is almost here! There are women in the party; so they do not come on the warpath. They must be looking for you. Hurry!"

Pierre needed no such warning, for, almost at Jacques' first words, he was crouching in one corner of the cabin, crawling under some old sacks, while Jacques was throwing a blanket and a coat over him. Then, piling some old shoes on top, and pulling up a bench in front of the spot, Jacques leaned over and whispered.

"I am going outside to take a look, but I will be right back."

With beating heart, Pierre made a small opening so he could peek out. He heard a sound. Someone was coming. Pierre watched the door. It was opening. He crouched as low as he could, smothering with the heat, and the excitement. But it was Jacques striding across the cabin. Pierre breathed once more. Jacque was picking up his musket.

"They are here!" he exclaimed. "If they come in, I will shoot them!"

"No, Jacques!" pleaded Pierre. "For my sake, do not start any trouble! That would be a terrible thing to do, for it would put the Indians on the warpath, and I would not want that. If I am well hidden and if no one tells that I am here, they will not find me. Why do you not go just outside the cabin, and pretend you are working. If you stand in the doorway with your musket, they will be sure to notice you are on guard."

Thoughtfully Jacques laid down his musket.

"You are right," he answered. "I will go outside — but will be very nearby." And he shut the cabin door.

Pierre crouched into as small a space as he could. His heart was pounding with excitement, and he was listening intently. Soon, he heard a commotion outside. The Indians must have arrived! It was very hot under the blankets, and outdoor sounds were muffled; but, even so, Pierre could not help hearing the clamor.

"Orimha! Orimha!" someone was shouting. Pierre listened. It was his sister's voice. "Orimha! Where are you?" This time it was his Indian mother. Then more and more voices took up the calling until it became a wailing chant. "Orimha! Where are you? Orimha! Orimha!"

For several hours this continued, while Pierre huddled, frightened and trembling, under the hot blanket. At last, the sounds began to die out. Sometime later, the door of the cabin was thrown open and Jacques rushed in.

"They have gone!" he cried. "You can come out now!"

Perspiring from the heat and the sudden relief, Pierre crawled out, and an excited Jacques threw his arms around him. Then he became thoughtful.

"You cannot stay here," he announced, "for they will surely be back again! The Governor said to come to his house tonight and we will see what can be done. These Indians thought a lot of you, didn't they? Do you know, one old woman cried!"

"That must have been my mother," Pierre replied, and he wiped away a sudden tear. "She was very good to me," he explained. Then, defensively, "But I had to get away, didn't I, Jacques?"

The Frenchman patted him on the back. "To be sure you did, my Pierre," he reassured him. "Come, let us hurry, for fear they return."

There were several at the Governor's home when Pierre and Jacques entered. Seated with the governor was a Jesuit Father, and a Dutchman. Jacques whispered to Pierre that this man was a rich merchant. Pierre took heart at seeing so many friends. The Governor was the first to speak.

"These friends are here to help you, Pierre," he explained. "We have been talking about sending you to New Amsterdam."

"New Amsterdam!" Pierre could not help exclaiming. "But that is south, and my people are to the north at Three Rivers."

"Yes," the Governor explained. "We know that, but Three Rivers is several hundred miles from here, through the woods. You do not know the way; we could not send enough men to protect you on such a long journey. You would be in constant danger of being captured again. You would not want that, would you, Pierre?"

Pierre shuddered at the thought and he shook his head in a violent "no."

Again the governor spoke.

"Soon, we are expecting a vessel from New Amsteram. When it sails, you will be on it. Once in New Amsterdam, you will be entirely safe from these Mohawks, and can await a boat going to Europe.

"Once in Europe, you can locate some ship which will be coming back to Canada, and you can reach your beloved family at Three Rivers."

Pierre was too overcome to speak for a moment. Sensing this, Jacques continued,

"It may seem a long way round to you, but, believe me, my Pierre, it is the only safe way."

Before Pierre could answer, the Jesuit Father stepped forward. "This is Father Honcet," the Governor explained. "He, too, was once captured by these same savages."

"My son," he said, "you have suffered much at the hands of these Indians. We must not let a Christian be captured by these savages again. I will confess you, and help you on your way. My earthly possessions are few, but I gladly give this to aid your departure." And he placed some gold pieces on the table.

Pierre's joy, as he comprehended all that this meant, was so great he hardly knew how to express himself. Murmuring his thanks to all of them, he threw himself at the Jesuit Father's feet, and said a prayer of gratitude.

The Jesuit Father spread out his hands in a benediction; and, for a few moments, the room was quiet. Then the merchant cleared his throat.

"I, too, wish to help; and I, myself, will arrange passage for you to New Amsteram."

At these words, everyone cheered, and Pierre poured out his gratitude to all.

Some time passed before the expected vessel arrived, but, knowing that his chances of getting back home were so good, Pierre enjoyed himself in the meantime. To the delight of the Dutch, he learned a few of their words. He helped them harvest their pumpkins and corn, and he joined them in their good times.

One evening, Jacques said to Pierre, "How would you like to club the cat tonght?"

Pierre was puzzled. "Club the cat?" he echoed.

Jacques laughed.

"We do not really hurt the creature — just scare him. Of course, the governor does not quite approve, so we go where he cannot see us, and we have several watching in case we need to be warned. Come, Pierre, do not be so startled. It is fun — you shall see!"

Together they went to the edge of the settlement, down by the great river where they joined a company of some ten or twelve young men.

"Here we are," announced Jacques. "You will see how we do this, and what sport it is."

Pierre, very much interested, watched while several young men drove two stout sticks into the ground. Between these, they stretched a strong rope, and, from the rope, suspended a barrel with its hoops slightly loosened. Then, two others came with a cat in an old sack.

To the great amusement of all, when they attempted to drop the cat into the barrel, he spat and clawed at them, and almost got away. But they finally managed to get him in, and to cover the opening to keep him there.

Having drawn straws to determine in which order each would take his turn, they armed themselves with stout sticks and lined up for the fun.

Pierre and Jacques were at the edge of the group watching. As each person's turn came, he stood at a given distance and threw his club as hard as he could at the suspended barrel. The first one to break the barrel and release the cat was the winner.

Once the poor cat was free, all the young men began to chase it. And what a tumult there was; as they followed it — darting in and out behind bushes and trees! Some of the young men bumped heads as they attempted to grasp the fleeing cat, and those who were watching poked fun at them.

After the game was over, the men wandered down by the river and smoked and visited. It had been fun to see the men "club the cat"; but, as he sat by the water's edge, Pierre could think only of how soon he might be sailing away on this very river. When would it be? And what lay ahead for him?

※　※　※　＊　※　＊

When, at length, a vessel did arrive, everyone at Fort Orange seemed to be interested in having Pierre get safely away. They could not do enough for him. They presented him with gifts; they prepared everything he might need for his journey. On the day when the vessel was to sail, many people came to see him off.

Now that he was really leaving, Pierre began to feel very bad over parting with these new-found friends. Tears came into his eyes, as he stood on shore and bade them goodbye. Jacques whispered,

"Goodbye, my friend, Pierre; I shall always remember you. May God grant that we meet again, sometime!"

Then Pierre entered the small boat with the sailors who were to row him out to the vessel, and, as they drew away from the shore, he waved to the friends he was leaving behind. Soon, he was climbing up the side of the vessel. The anchor was raised, the wind fluttered, then caught the sails, and they were off. As he stood on the afterdeck and waved for the last time at the now miniature figures on shore, his heart swelled within him as he wondered if he would ever see any of them again. Then his thoughts turned toward the future. What further adventures lay ahead of him?

Now they were sailing down the great river between beautifully rolling hills. All the long distance to New Amsterdam, Pierre enjoyed the view as the river narrowed or widened. Then the surrounding hills grew higher and higher, until they were veritable mountains.

But at last, the great river widened once more; the mountains changed to hills, and, suddenly, New Amsterdam came into view.

As they were dropping anchor near another vessel already in the harbor, Pierre eagerly scanned the fortress of New Amsterdam with its Dutch flag flying in the breeze. As he fingered a letter to the governor, Peter Stuyvesant, from the governor at Fort Orange, Pierre could hardly contain his eagerness to get ashore and to make arrangements for his passage back to Europe. Would it be on this vessel near which they had anchored?

*　　*　　*　　*　　*

Some days later, Pierre was standing on the deck of another vessel which was on its way across the Atlantic. A soft breeze billowed the sails, and the sun danced upon the crests of the waves. As he watched the shore line grow dimmer and dimmer, Pierre thought with gratitude of his friends at Fort Orange and of those who had aided him at New Amsterdam. During the long voyage, he spent much of his time thinking about his experiences with the Indians.

"I have been one of the Mohawks," he mused. "I have seen the land of the Oneidas, the Senecas, and the Onondagas. I have been past the great falls to the west, and seen land which no white man has ever beheld. And even though I am on my way back to Europe, some day, I feel I will return to these lands and travel again where these Indians live."

*　　*　　*　　*　　*

The ship which was carrying Pierre back to Europe was a Dutch vessel, and so it was that Pierre landed in Holland. From here, he had to find his way back to his native France. Once in his own country, and working as he could, he constantly planned how to return to his own people across the ocean.

Winter arrived and once more, the time dragged for Pierre. But, when May came, he managed to be on the high seas heading again, for the New World. Most of the days during the voyage he spent impatiently walking the deck, or leaning on the railing, watching the rolling waves and listening to the creaking of the ship's rigging. But, as they drew nearer and nearer the end of the trip, he spent many long intervals straining his eyes for the first dark line on the far horizon which would mean land. And how excited he and all the rest of the passengers were when, as last, they reached the safety of the St. Lawrence River!

It was pleasant sailing up the river, but Pierre could hardly wait for the vessel to anchor off Quebec, and for the small boats to take them ashore.

Once on land, he began searching for some friendly Indians who might be heading for Three Rivers. At last, when he had found some, he eagerly offered to help them load their canoes and get started.

As he paddled in unison with his Indian companions, Pierre thought of all the long months of waiting since he had left New Amsterdam. It hardly seemed possible that, once more, he was so close to home. How would he find everything at Three Rivers? Would his people be all right? He shuddered at the thought that anything could have happened to them. Two years was a long time to have been away! But he must not think of such things! Now, he must be happy! And, with a vigorous stroke of his paddle, he burst into song. The Indians caught the spirit, and joined in; and, laughing as they glided on, they came, at length, within sight of Three Rivers.

As the walls of the stockade appeared through the trees, Pierre's eagerness and joy forced him to paddle more rapidly than ever. Laughing, the savages kept pace with his strokes.

Now, they were in shallow water; now, the canoe was touching the shore. And Pierre, pouring out his thanks to the Indians, was rushing up the bank, through the long grass, to the southeast gate of the fortress.

At the entrance, an armed guard challenged him. Pierre hurried up to him.

"Monsieur Pepin," he exclaimed, "do you not know me? I am Pierre Radisson!"

For an instant, Monsieur Pepin stared at him from under puzzled brows. Then, dropping his musket, "Mon Dieu!" he shouted. "It is indeed you, Pierre!"

Grasping Pierre by the arm, he almost dragged him inside the gateway. Leaning in the doorway of the nearest cabin, a man was smoking. Monsieur Pepin called to him, "Bertrand Fafard, come see! Pierre Radisson is back!" Monsieur Fafard almost dropped his pipe in astonished recognition, as he hurried toward them. While running, he called to others; and, in no time at all, Pierre, entirely surrounded by excited men, women, children, and barking dogs, was hurrying past the familiar home of the Jesuits, down St. Louis Street, toward his own home. Someone from the crowd ran ahead, so that by the time he and his companions were within sight of his cabin, his mother, father, and his sister, Margaret, were rushing out the doorway.

They threw their arms around him. They all wept, unashamed; and his mother kept repeating over and over ,"Is it truly you, Pierre? Is it truly you?" — while she stroked his head to see if he were real.

For several days there was great rejoicing at Three Rivers. All the settlement came to hear how Pierre had escaped from the Indians. Part of his time he spent in getting acquainted with his new brother-in-law, for Margaret had married Medard Chouart while Pierre had been gone. Everywhere he went, little knots of people gathered to ask him about the fierce Iroquois, to beg him to tell, again, his adventurous story; or to ask him to speak in the Mohawk tongue.

No matter how many times Pierre repeated his story, they never seemed to tire of it. As for Pierre, he was content for a long time, just to enjoy the sight of his mother and sister going about their daily tasks; or to be with his father; or to wander up and down the streets of Three Rivers and enjoy to the fullest the feeling that, miraculously, he was once more back home.

But, sometimes, he stood at the southeast gate of the stockade and gazed out across the broad expanse of the St. Lawrence River; and, even as on that long ago May morning, he wondered about the land beyond the horizon. Would he ever again visit it?

CHAPTER XV

The seasons passed quickly for Pierre. A second spring rolled around, and another, and yet a third. Again it was spring, and again Pierre had begun to grow restless after the long confinement of a cold winter.

One June morning, as he and his family were seated at the breakfast table, a neighbor burst in.

"Monsieur Radisson," he addressed Pierre's father, "Father Ragueneau and Father DuPeron have come from Quebec, and they want to see Pierre. Even now, they are almost here."

A look of apprehension crossed Madame Radisson's face.

"What do you suppose they want of Pierre?" she asked. Then, "Come, Margaret," she said to her daughter. "Let us put on two more plates for our guests."

As she spoke, there was a knock at the door. Pierre's father hurried to open it.

"Good morning, Fathers," he greeted the two priests, who stood there. "Do come in!"

The two fathers bowed to all the family, and, for a few moments after they were seated, they chatted about the weather and the crops. Then one, Father Ragueneau, turned toward Pierre.

"My son," he said, "we know that you have lived with the Mohawk Indians, and, therefore, you know them. Your people may have told you that while you were away, one of our brothers, Father Le Moyne, explored the land of the Onondagas,, who are the western neighbors of the Mohawks. Later several of our Jesuit Fathers, and some fifty Frenchmen went to that land, and built a chapel and a fort."

"Yes, Father," Pierre answered, "I have heard of this settlement."

Father Ragueneau continued.

"Now, there are here among us some Indians from the Onondagans and some from the Senecas. They are asking that we go back with them to establish a colony, and take, also, some of our friendly Huron Indians with us. We have deliberated for a long time, while they grow impatient. Now, they are saying that if we do not go soon, they will return to their own lands, and they will kill all of our people who are in the fort, and at the mission."

Pierre's mother leaned forward.

"Do you really think they would?" she asked.

"Yes," answered Pierre. "From what I have seen of them, I would say they would."

Father Ragueneau looked long and earnestly at Pierre.

"We must do something quickly," he said. "and, Pierre, we need your help! Our own French people in the land of the Onondagas must be protected. Also, we of the Church wish to convert these savages to Christian ways; and we have pledged ourselves to this work, even if it takes our lives. We have nineteen Frenchmen and about one hundred Hurons who are ready to accompany us. We need someone who knows the ways of the Indians and can speak their language. You can help us. Will you do it? Searchingly, he gazed into Pierre's eyes. "Will you go with us?" he pleaded.

Before answering, Pierre glanced questioningly at his mother and father. "What do you think?" he asked.

He saw his mother crush one corner of her apron in her hand; but she said nothing. His father thoughtfully tapped a spoon on the table. Then he rose and looked down into Pierre's upturned face.

"My son," he said, "you are a man now, and I should not make your decisions for you. Naturally, we would like to have you stay with us; but, as the Father says, our people need help; and the Church has work to do. You must decide for yourself."

For a moment, Pierre hesitated. Then, turning to Father Ragueneau, "I will let you know this afternoon," he said, and, when their guests had departed, he went outside, and walked up and down thinking what he should do.

After the family had finished its mid-day meal, Pierre rose from the table and stood with his hands on his mother's shoulder.

"I think I will go," he announced, quietly. "We should be a large enough party to protect ourselves; and I have learned that the fortress in the Onondaga country is of a good size, and well-built. I know how to travel through the woods, and how to speak the Iroquois tongue. Perhaps I can help our people."

Pierre's mother put his hand to her lips, and he could feel the hot tears on her face.

"If you must go, take care of yourself," she whispered.

Pierre's father gripped his other hand hard.

And, so it was that a little later, Pierre was setting out once more for the land of the fierce Iroquois. Having made the decision to go, Pierre felt almost happy at the thought of starting out on an adventure. But, now that the actual time of leaving had arrived, his heart was heavy as he said goodbye to his bravely-smiling family. Back of his father's hearty handclasp, his mother's tight embrace, and his sister Margaret's kiss, he knew the courage they had summoned to keep back the tears.

As Pierre was waving a last farewell to his family and friends gathered by the riverbank, his own heart became heavy with apprehension. How would this adventure end? Had he done the right thing to set out on this journey? But he had given his promise. He could not turn back! Resolutely, he dipped his paddle into the water in time with those of the other Frenchmen in the canoe. And they shot out from shore to join the picturesque convoy of Indians and whites on the broad-blue expanse of the forest-lined river.

From the very start, however, Pierre had a feeling which, try as he might to shake off, he could not — a feeling that this was to be a dangerous and unhappy trip. To begin with, it was very hot. This made the paddling of the heavily-laden canoes difficult. After a time, they came to rapids, and the canoes and baggage had to be laboriously hauled overland, through the forest, past these dangerous spots. Many of the party grew weary and lagged behind. Some even expressed the wish to turn back.

At length, a wide part of the river was reached, and, Pierre, ever watchful, noticed that the Onondagas were making the Hurons transfer to their canoes, and were paddling away with them. Sensing danger, Pierre and his companions paddled alongside the canoe in which were Father Ragueneau and Father DuPeron.

"Father," Pierre said. "These Onondagas are not to be trusted. Even now, they are forcing the Hurons to go off with them."

"So!" exclaimed the Father. "Who will go with us after them?"

Pierre's canoe and several others joined Father Raguenau and Father DuPeron. And, when they had caught up with the Onondagas, Father Ragueneau was very stern. He spoke in loud and impressive tones.

"You say that you want peace; that you love the Huron. What does this mean?"

When they saw how angry the Frenchmen were, the Onondagas pretended to be very friendly; but Pierre was not convinced they meant it. He remembered how, back at Three Rivers, the canoe in which Father Ragueneau was to embark had been so loaded by the Onondagas that there had been no room for the Father. When Father Ragueneau had protested, the Onondagas had pretended that it was a mistake. But was it? Just how dangerous a situation were they getting into?

All went well for several days after this. Then, one evening, as they were making camp, to his horror, Pierre saw an Onondaga suddenly knife a Huron in the back. Pierre called to the other Frenchmen. But his cries were drowned out by the sudden, blood-curling yells of the Onondagas, as, with

107

flying tomahawks, and murderous knives, they leaped at the surprised Hurons. Quickly dropping the firewood they were gathering, and grabbing up their muskets, the white men hurried to prevent the massacre. But, since the Huron Indians had chosen a camp site a little distant from the white men, all the Huron men were killed by the time they reached them.

As they took a stand in front of the bleeding corpses of the Huron men, and the huddled forms of the frightened women and children, Father Ragueneau's eyes flashed angrily. Accusingly, he shook his raised fist at the guilty Onondagas standing with their still-bloody weapons in their hands.

"How good is the word of the Onondaga?" he thundered. "You say you will take us and our Huron friends safely to your land. But you do not. You kill many of our friends. How can you do such a thing?"

The wind blew Father Ragueneau's black robe about his spare figure. He lowered his voice to a steady, impassioned tone. His eyes became slits in his set, and angry face. He pounded his chest with his clenched fist.

"These blows have rent my heart! I cannot restrain my tears at this horrible sight, for these Hurons were like my children to me. How could a father and mother see their children killed without sharing their sufferings? I have the tenderness of a mother, and the heart of a father for these, my poor Christian Hurons."

He raised his voice in a mighty shout.

"How could you do this to my children?"

He pounded his chest with both fists.

"Burn me! Yes, even kill me, if you will. But let them live!"

He glanced compassionately down at the dead men at his feet.

"Willingly would I suffer, if by this, I could bring them back to life. But, since that is impossible, I have these words to carry to you."

Taking a few steps toward the defiant Onondagas, he threw wampum at their feet, and spoke in a loud, authoritative voice.

"First, you must hold your fury and stay your hatchets. No more do you continue to vent your cruelty on these Huron women and children who are left. Too much innocent blood has been spilled. God, who has seen your wickedness, will take vengeance upon you if you anger him again."

He threw more wampum in front of the Onondagas, and continued in a loud voice.

"Second, these Huron women and children must be considered as your own people, and treated kindly."

Again, Father Ragueneau cast wampum at their feet. Staring piercingly at the Onondagas, he shouted.

"Third, we will continue on our journey as if nothing had happened, but the white men will not forget this deed. Let there be no more of it. I have spoken."

And he took a few steps back to where his fellow Frenchmen were standing.

Then the captain of the Onondagas stepped forward, and, with folded arms, and in an arrogant tone, he addressed Father Ragueneau.

"The Onondagas keep their word. We love our Huron brothers. It was your governor, and your Father Mercier who told us to do this. We only obey the white man's orders."

Father Ragueneau shook his fist at the captain of the Onondagas.

"You lie!" he shouted. "This is not true!"

But the Indian captain merely half-smiled as he said, "The black robe does not know all that I know."

Unflinchingly, Father Ragueneau stood his ground.

"That is a poor excuse! I know my own French people. And I know this is not true. There is to be no more bloodshed. The white men have spoken!"

Turning away from the Onondagas, he joined Father DuPeron who was administering the last rites of the church to the fallen Hurons.

That night, the Onondaga captain came to Father Ragueneau. Throwing down some wampum, he spoke,

"The Onondaga has nothing crooked in his thoughts. He wishes to be thy brother. Turn away the muzzles of thy fire arms from the bodies of the Onondagas."

Father Ragueneau regarded him severely. Then, he, too, threw down a piece of wampum and said,

"The white man wishes to live in peace with his red brother."

The Onondaga captain threw down more wampum.

"I cast into the depths of the earth all mutual reproach," he answered.

Pierre was relieved to hear these words. Nevertheless, he and the rest of the white people took council, and decided they would take turns being on watch for the rest of the journey.

CHAPTER XVI

Some days later, the party reached the Thousand Islands, and discovered other Indians making camp.

"Let us see who they are," Pierre said to Father Ragueneau. As they approached, Pierre exclaimed, "They are Mohawks! I know some of them!"

When the Mohawks recognized Pierre, they crowded round him.

"Orimha!" they exclaimed. "Where have you been? Where did you go? Do you come back to your people? Your mother and father have mourned a long time for you."

Pierre had to think quickly. He did not want the Indians to learn that the kindly Dutch had helped him to escape, for the Indians might be angry and cause them harm, so he answered,

"I hunted in the woods; and, in twelve days came near Three Rivers; so I stopped to visit the French."

"You come back now?" the Mohawks persisted.

Pierre put them off.

"I visit my friends. Later I will come. Are my father and mother and brother and sisters well?"

The Mohawks assured him that they were. Pierre was relieved to learn that his foster father had not been killed by the French. Going to his pack, he returned with some knives and brass rings.

"Here are gifts for my family. You will take them?" he asked.

The Mohawks were pleased.

That evening, the Mohawks had a feast, and Pierre was relieved when they departed the next morning.

A few days later, Pierre and his party reached Lake Ontario, and, finally, a river. After they had gone for some time on this river, they paddled out onto a small lake. A beautifully-wooded shore line, and distant, rolling hills added to the attractiveness of the landscape.

The canoe of the Onondaga captain was paddled over to Father Ragueneau.

"It is not far, now." he assured the Father.

Pierre was glad to hear this. How good it would be to reach the protecting walls of the fortress, and to feel safe once more!

Soon, the Onondagas were heading their canoes toward shore. And, through the trees, Pierre could see the cross-topped watch tower of the fortress. All gave a lusty shout. There was an answering cry from the fortress. As their canoes grounded, and they stepped out, the French from the fortress were there; some even wading out into the water to greet them. They threw their arms around them and cried,

"Welcome!" "Welcome to the fort and chapel of Sainte Marie de Gannentaha!"

On the rise of ground before them, the fort's walls of pointed-tipped logs rose, and Pierre's heart was grateful at their promise of protection. But before climbing to the entrance, Father Ragueneau and Father DuPeron paused to thank God for their safe arrival.

(A replica of this chapel and fortress has been built on the original site along the shores of Onondaga Lake near Syracuse, New York.)

At the double gateway entrance, the commander, Monsieur du Puys, greeted the party. His joy at their arrival soon dispelled any sense of formality; and he and the nine soldiers on duty with him were soon making the newcomers comfortable, offering them food, and showing them about the fortress.

They walked around the walled enclosure and examined the soldiers' barracks, the carpenter's shop, the bake shop, with its open fireplace and side oven, the large bellows in the blacksmith's shop, and the Jesuit Chapel opposite the front gate. Pierre was interested in the defenses, too, so he climbed the ladder to the top of the lookout tower which commanded a panoramic view of the lake and the surrounding hills. He walked up the ramps to the raised platforms built against the inside walls of the fort, taking note of how well planned were the openings through which muskets might be fired from above the heads of any approaching enemy.

Having examined the inside of the fortress, Pierre and a few others walked outside and saw the cleared land where corn and turnips had been planted, and where many fat hogs rooted inside a fenced enclosure. Nearby, the Huron women and children were making camp, and, to Pierre's surprise, the Onondagas, also, seemed to be settling down. Pierre turned to one of the soldiers.

"Do the Onondagas live here?" he asked.

"No," the man replied. "Their village is some distance away."

Pierre said no more, but he pondered about the matter for several days. He became more and more apprehensive as the Onondagas remained encamped in such a way that they entirely surrounded the fortress.

At last, Pierre took council with Monsieur du Puys and Father Regueneau.

"I do not like it," he said. "These Onondagas are not as friendly as they pretend. We must watch them."

Captain du Puys sighed.

"I think you are right," he replied. "We will have to give them presents, and try to keep them happy. Perhaps, then, they will be satisfied, and will not make trouble."

The weeks went quickly by. Sometimes the white men fished in the lake for salmon; sometimes they hunted nearby. Summer waned, and autumn set in. Still the Onondaga encampment surrounded the French fortress, like a besieging army. Many of these Indians had even erected bark cabins.

One morning Pierre went to Monsieur du Puys.

"Sir," he said, "last night, I heard the Indians singing war songs. I went outside the fortress walls and watched.

Some were dancing and breaking kettles with their hatchets. That means war, sir."

A soldier standing nearby spoke up,

"Last night some Mohawks joined the camp."

Pierre and Monsieur du Puys murmured in alarm.

"I will go outside," Pierre said, "and talk with them. Perhaps I can learn something."

When he came back, the men clustered about him.

"Did you find out anything?"

Pierre shook his head.

"These Mohawks are not from my village; and they would tell me nothing."

Father Ragueneau spoke up.

"We had best send a message back to Quebec asking for aid. Perhaps we can ward off an attack until help arrives."

"Let us all go!" cried one Frechman.

"Yes, let us!" Many more joined in, excitedly.

But when Father Ragueneau answered them, his voice was tinged with anger.

"Would you expose yourselves to capture? The moment we all go from this fortress, the Indians will follow us and try to massacre us. Here in the fortress, we have protection. Out there, we would have nothing. It is growing cold; and very soon it will be too cold for a large party to travel. Besides that, most of the boats in which we came belonged to the Indians. We have not enough for everyone to escape and to carry enough supplies for the long journey. Many of our canoes have been smashed."

Pierre nodded his agreement.

"You are right, Father. We are much safer here for the present, but we must have help. Some messengers could steal away and get through when a large party could not."

Two French soldiers stepped forward.

"We know this country; we will go," they said.

Eleven more soldiers, and one Jesuit joined the group.

Several months dragged by, each one seeming to bring an Indian war nearer and nearer. Larger and larger parties of Mohawks arrived to join those already besieging the fortress, until at last there were four hundred in the bark cabins which entirely surrounded the fortress. The French were greatly worried.

"We must do something," they all said. "What has become of our messengers? Something must have happened to them. Perhaps no help will come!"

Monsieur du Puys raised his hands to silence them,

"Let us make ready to help ourselves. We can build boats inside the fortress where the Indians cannot see us. Perhaps, if we are ready, an opportunity will come."

"That is a good idea," the rest agreed. "Let us get to work on them at once."

And everyone who was not busy at something else, set about the task. No Indians were allowed within the fortress while this work was going on; and the boats were hidden when they were not being worked on.

Every night, the Indians became louder and louder in their songs and dances, working themselves into frenzy. And frequently they appeared decked in full war paint. No Frenchman went outside the fortress during the day, and none dared to go out after dark. Guards were posted at all times.

One day, a Huron slave came to the fortress gates with some corn.

"I would come in," he said to the guard.

Seeing he was alone, the guard asked him to wait for a little while. And, calling several other guards to watch, he hurried to warn all those who were working on the boats and canoes.

"Hide everything, quickly," he cautioned. "There is a Huron slave who wants to come in. I think he has been sent to spy. If I tell him 'no', then the Indians will guess what we are doing. Hurry to put everything away! We must fool him!"

115

When the Huron was allowed to enter the fortress, he presented some corn which he carried; and the French gave him gifts to take back to the Onondagas who owned him.

All the next day, Pierre thought and thought about their desperate situation; and he was troubled that the guard had allowed the Huron slave to come inside the fortress. Perhaps the slave might have seen something to make him suspicious. Pierre knew that the boats were almost completed — good, strong, flat-bottomed ones that would carry fifteen or sixteen men. If only they could get away soon!

But it was still late winter; and the lake was frozen. How could they travel? And, even if navigation were possible, how could they leave without being seen by the Indians?

The next day Pierre was still pondering the problem. Perhaps he should go outside the fortress to see if he knew any of the Mohawk Indians who had come recently. If he could find any from his adopted tribe, he might get some information from them. After an hour outside, he returned, and went at once to Father Ragueneau.

"Father," he said, "I have been outside the fortress."

"Alone?" asked the Father.

"Yes, alone."

"You should not have done that. It is not safe."

"It was all right. I wanted to see if there were any Mohawks I knew."

"And were there?"

"Yes, Father, I found my foster Indian father."

Father Ragueneau glanced up in surprise.

"What did he say, Pierre?"

"He wanted me to stay with them. I had to tell him something, so I said I was visiting my French friends, and, someday, I would go back to the Mohawk country."

Father Ragueneau frowned.

"Did he seem satisfied?"

"Yes, and he was glad to see me. But he tells me the Huron slave says we are building a boat, so he must have seen something, after all."

"That is bad," replied the Father.

"It could be," agreed Pierre, "but, fortunately, this Huron has been baptized, and he knows some Bible stories. When he saw the boat, he went back and told the Mohawks that there was to be a great flood, for he had seen the boat which the French were building to escape in; but that all the Indians would be drowned."

Father Ragueneau smiled.

"Did the Mohawks believe this?"

"They are not sure; and my father tells me they will send scouts to visit us," answered Pierre.

Father Rageneau pondered for a few minutes. "I think we could hide the boats in the chapel, and build a floor over them. Then, when the scouts come, we will be sure they visit all parts of the fortress. When they see nothing of any boats, they will believe the Huron lied, because he is not one of their own people."

It was Pierre's turn to smile. "That will be good," he said.

Father Ragueneau questioned him further.

"What else did you learn?"

A worried look crossed Pierre's face.

"My foster father tells me the Mohawks wish to make war now, and that it is only the Onondagas who keep them from fighting. He said I should come with him and be his son once more, for they are going to attack soon, anyway."

"Why did the Onondagas stop the Mohawks from attacking? And why did they ask us here in the first place if they did not want us?" asked Father Rageneau.

"He says that the Onondagas did not want us here," Pierre replied, "but they thought, if we come, we could get the Hurons they want to kill. The only reason they have not attacked us is because they have heard that our French people at Quebec hold some of the Onondagas as hostages, since the Onondagas did some killing after we left. The Onondagas are afraid if they attack us, that our people back home will hear of it, and will kill these hostages. But my father says that the

Mohawks are going to attack us soon, anyway. It is a very bad situation," concluded Pierre, "and we must get away."

"Yes, but how?" the Father asked. "We are surrounded on all sides by hostile Indians. The ice is not yet out of the lake. And, if we tried to steal out by night, we would be followed and attacked. What could save us? Surely, we are better off to remain here."

"Yes," said Pierre. "It does seem hopeless to think of escaping. But, while my Indian father was talking, I had a sudden idea. From living with the Indians, I know that they are great believers in dreams. It is almost a religious requirement that they do whatever an Indian dreams they should do."

"I had not heard that," replied the Father. "You have some plan?"

"Yes, I could tell my Indian father that I have had a dream. I could say that I have dreamed that we should give a great feast to our Indian friends — an 'Eat-all' feast as they call it. They will be pleased, and they can not refuse to obey my dream, for I am one of them by adoption."

"Then we will cook all the food we can lay our hands on. They will not attack us before the party. And, by taking as much time as possible to prepare this feast, we can delay the war."

Father Ragueneau interrupted.

"But how will this feasting help us to escape?"

"Do you not see?" said Pierre. "We will fill them so full that they will fall into a stupor, and we can steal away. Perhaps, in a few days the ice will begin to break up."

But Father Ragueneau was not convinced.

"How can we be sure they will eat so much?" he asked.

"Never fear," replied Pierre. "I know they will! For every Iroquois Indian is taught that when he is a guest at an 'Eat-all' feast, he must eat everything that is placed before him. Just like obeying the dream, it is practically a religious duty."

Father Ragueneau smiled his relief. "I think you have a good idea, Pierre," he said. "We will see what Monsieur du Puys and the others think."

When they told them of Pierre's plan, all were hopeful for the first time in months.

"Let us try it!" they cried. "We should be able to fool these savages."

"Yes," said another. "We can seat all these savages in front of the fortress; and some of us could play loud music and dance and sing while the Indians are eating. Then, we can carry out the boats and supplies at the rear of the fort and they will not hear us!"

"And another thing," cried someone else, "We could stuff some dummies and put them up in place of the sentries. That might be good, too. If we can get the Indians to eat themselves into a stupor, they would not guess we were not here."

And the men laughed.

"I know," grinned another soldier. "We could tie the chapel bell cord to the leg of a pig. If we scatter corn on the ground, the pig will move about, and make the bell ring. Then the Indians will think we are still here. Think of the head start we could have before they discover we are gone! I guess that would be a good joke on them."

The men were all jubilant.

"Let us try all of these things!" they exclaimed.

And so, Pierre told his Indian father of his dream; and, when the news had spread among the Indians, they were pleased. They wanted to come inside the fortress to see how the French were preparing this great feast; but the French told them it was not customary to let their guests see any of the feast until it was all ready.

Meanwhile, the French were hurrying to pack their baggage in preparation for a hasty departure, and they were also cooking most of the food they had on hand.

Like little children, the Indians kept asking when the feast would be ready. Day by day, the French put them off, thinking to make them hungrier, so they would be all the more willing to eat heartily. Also they knew that the longer they delayed, the more chance there was that the ice in the lake would begin to break up, and they could use their boats.

Each man in the fortress worked feverishly at his appointed task. Some caught and prepared the fish; some baked corn meal biscuits; some prepared great kettles of bear's meat and turtle soup. Knowing what food would please the Indians, Pierre helped with this work.

Finally, the day of the great feast arrived. The impatient Indians had made such a clamor that the French could put them off no longer. The ice in the lake had become honeycombed, and the white men decided they must take a chance on getting away. Toward the end of the afternoon, the French saw that all the Indians were seated on the hillside in front of the fort, and, with their backs to the water. At the entrance to the stockade, a bugler stood, and, just as the gates were being thrown open, he blew several mighty blasts on his trumpet.

An awed and deadly silence fell on the assembled Indians. Then, through the gates came twenty-four Frenchmen bending under the great weight of twelve kettles of stewed meat, and bearing hundreds of cornmeal biscuits. And, behind them, came more Frenchmen singing, dancing, shouting, and blowing trumpets. The din was terrific.

When the Indians saw so much food, their eyes fairly popped from their heads. One old warrior stood up, and, although he could not be heard above the tumult, he gave thanks to his gods that the generous French had come to honor them so.

The Frenchmen passed among the Indians and offered all some of the feast. Like greedy animals, the Indians fell on the kettles of food. They grabbed tasty portions and stuffed themselves, grunting their satisfaction, licking their fingers, and smacking their lips. There were kettles of ducks, turkeys, salmon, carp and eels. But best of all the pleasing dishes were the kettles of turtles, for the Indians believed because turtles were long in dying, that anyone who ate their meat would be hard to kill. Knowing this, Pierre had urged the French to prepare this favorite dish.

Throughout the feast, many of the Frenchmen continued dancing and singing, and making all the clamor they could. Catching the spirit, some of the Indians themselves, also danced and sang.

For a time, the Indians smacked their lips and kept repeating, "Am I really eating?" But, when the French brought on more and more food — bear, mush, and venison, the Indians began to show signs of feeling uncomfortable.

"Give them more, and still more!" Pierre kept whispering to his fellow countrymen. But they needed no urging, for they were beginning to see the chance of Pierre's plot really working. They noticed that the Indians were evidently forcing themselves to put more food into their mouths, even though they could hardly swallow. The French carried out more steaming kettles, and still more — until even the Indians could no longer fulfill their sacred obligation. As Pierre and his companions reappeared with yet more steaming food, many Indians began to shake their heads. Some rolled on the ground in their distress, and, soon, many were calling, "Skegon!" which meant enough. But the French had no mercy.

Pierre stood before the Indians.

"Surely you have not had enough!" he exclaimed. "Your white brothers are used to giving very large feasts for their friends; and we have much more for you!"

At these words, other Indians groaned and called, "Skegon!" in weak tones. Many lay on the ground, some writhing in agony, some almost in a stupor.

Glancing at these prostrate ones, Pierre suggested, "Perhaps you would like to sleep before you eat more."

Gratefully, the Indians who were able, cried, "We sleep, we sleep!" and immediately stretched themselves out on the ground.

It had grown so dark by this time that Pierre could barely pick out some of the dark forms against the snow.

Smiling to himself, he announced, loudly, "And we will sleep for a while, too."

When all of the Indians had lain down, Pierre and the rest of the white men hurried inside the fortress.

"Is everything ready?" they asked eagerly.

"Yes," replied Monsieur du Puys and Father Ragueneau.

"The loaded boats and canoes are already in the lake. We have smashed our extra firearms, and have scattered in the snow the ammunition we could not carry. And we have put up the dummy sentinels. How is it outside? Is it safe to go yet?"

Before Pierre could reply, some of the soldiers stepped forward. "Why do we not kill all these savages while we have the chance? It would be easy while they are all so stupefied."

"Yes," chimed in another. "Then there would be just women and children and old men left in their villages. We could kill them easily enough. If we kill off all these Indians, perhaps we could live in peace!"

"That is a good idea!" others cried. "Let us do it before we go!"

But Father Ragueneau and Father DuPeron were horrified. "No!" they said firmly. "We cannot permit such an unchristian deed!"

"But, they have killed so many of our people!" protested one soldier. "This would end their killings!"

Father Ragueneau looked very stern.

"To begin with, there are other tribes elsewhere, so you could not possibly kill them all by murdering these. Besides that, we could never agree to this deed of revenge," he said. "The cross must be our sword!"

Then Pierre spoke up. "Let us be off," he suggested. "We could not hope to exterminate all these Indians. If we kill some Mohawks, and some Onondagas, all of the rest of the Iroquois will be on the warpath. It would only make things worse for us; and now, we are losing valuable time. Let us get away while we can. Every minute is precious."

"He is right," said Monsieur du Puys. "Let us go quickly!"

"It is half after ten o'clock," one of the soldiers said. "We had better put all the distance we can between us and these Indians before daylight."

Hastily, but quietly, the men chained shut the front gate of the fortress and then crept outside and down to the water's edge. The last one to go through the hole in the fortress wall was Pierre. In the darkness, he strained his eyes to see if all seemed well. Silhouetted against the sky he could discern the dummies placed to represent guards; and he could hear the pig sniffing the ground as it moved about, feeding on the corn. As the pig moved, the chapel bell rang, lazily, because of the rope fastened to its leg.

With one last look at what he could see in the darkness, Pierre turned and followed the rest down to the water's edge. How long would it be before they would again be protected by such a fortress? As he crammed himself into the tightly-packed canoe, Pierre shivered with apprehension.

He strained his ears for any frightening sounds behind them; but there were none. Tense and quiet, the men were pushing the boats and canoes away from the shore. It was dark and cold. A bitter breeze blew across the lake from the snow-covered hills. There were blocks of ice floating, ghost-like, in the lake; and, as the wind hit the water, it froze a thin skin of ice on its surface.

Now and again, the men muttered under their breath as an unseen cake of ice almost smashed their canoe. But, for the most part, they paddled silently through the dark night, urged on by desperate necessity, and straining every nerve to listen for any warning of pursuing savages. But the only sounds were the quiet gurgling of the paddles, the heavy breathing of the men, and the thin tinkling of breaking ice as they pushed steadily ahead.

For a while, an occasional breeze carried the muted sound of the chapel bell to their straining ears. And, as he listened, each man had the same thought to urge him on. They must get away from that sound! For, what chance had fifty-three Frenchmen against several hundred Indians?

All night long, and all the next day, the desperate men paddled without stopping. Their backs and their arms ached. And their eyes were red and strained from lack of sleep. But they knew they must keep paddling. Once or twice in the night, they saw remote camp fires glinting through the dense forest. As noiselessly as possible, they paddled on.

At last, they reached the river which emptied into Lake Ontario. But here, they met further obstacles — waterfalls and gushing rapids. In one spot, the swollen river was very narrow, with precipices on each side, from which they could easily have been ambushed. This meant they would have to land and carry their boats, canoes, and baggage through the dense wilderness. Pierre kept track of the time — four precious hours! By now, the Indians must surely be on their trail! But dead tired though the Frenchmen were, they could take no time to rest.

At length, the weary men came in sight of Lake Ontario. As they reached the ice-jammed mouth of the river, and gazed eagerly ahead, their spirits dropped, for the lake was still frozen; and there was no one among them who did not realize the delay that meant. However, this was no time to bemoan their fate.

"Come," said Father Ragueneau. "Let us cut our way through."

And, with clubs and hatchets, the men made passageways to float the boats and canoes. It was a slow and tedious business; but the men kept doggedly at it; and, upon reaching the St. Lawrence River, they were rewarded by the sight of open water.

Here, after two days of comparatively easy navigation, Pierre felt heartened for the first time.

"I think something must have happened to delay the Indians," he said to Father Ragueneau that night. "Perhaps they were too sick; or a storm may have hindered them. By now, we can hope to be safe."

"Whatever it was," replied the Father, "we should be giving thanks to the Lord for saving us."

Those who were nearby gave murmurs of assent.

But, contrary to Pierre's hopes, all their troubles were not yet over; for, on the next day, the party reached a great waterfall where some of them were nearly drowned. As if nature had not done enough to them, a little later, the rapids of the swollen river presented a greater hazard than any previous one. As they faced the sight of this violent current, the men's faces were set. Huge breakers extended all the way across the entire width of the rapids, and the water swirled in eddies, around large, partially-submerged rocks.

Monsieur du Puys glanced anxiously at Father Ragueneau and at Pierre. Then, without a word, he headed his canoe into the terrifying, broiling current. Taking firm grips on their paddles, the rest followed. With each stroke of the paddles, the angry waters, seemingly mountain high, forced the canoes into a whirling abyss. The men cried out at their own help-lessness, as the canoes were dashed against large rocks. Then, caught by the violence of the current, they were hurled, miraculously, away.

The shallow, flat-bottomed boats shipped water, and it looked as if any minute they might be swamped. Suddenly, above the roar of the rapids, came cries of "Help!" And, in the one fleeting second as the canoe in which he was riding whirled in the current, Pierre saw one of the canoes over-turned, and its occupants thrown into the icy, churning waters.

Desperately, all those who were nearby strove to reach them, but they could not. As the upturned canoe swirled within reach of one of the men, he managed to grasp it, but the force of the current swept it toward a falls on the edge of the rapids.

Pierre caught another fleeting glimpse of Monsieur du Puys' canoe as it leaped toward the falls. And then, the rest of the canoes and boats were shooting over in rapid succession.

Miraculously, they came to rest in the river below the falls. And it was not until then that they perceived that Monsieur du Puys and his companions had managed to save the one who had clung to the overturned canoe.

Exhausted, the man slumped in front of Monsieur du Puys.

"He was about ready to give up when we reached him," called Monsieur du Puys.

Father Ragueneau cupped his hands and called across to him, "Where are the other three?"

For an answer, Monsieur du Puys shook his head sadly.

It was nearly two weeks later that the weary and be-draggled party came within sight of Montreal. Guards posted near the river sighted them, and kind hands helped them from their boats.

"Thank God, we have reached safety!" exclaimed Father Ragueneau as they were being taken inside the houses and given food and dry clothing. And all the party joined in this feeling of deep gratitude.

The inhabitants of Montreal could not do enough for the travelers.

"You must stay awhile," they said.

But Monsieur du Puys protested.

"We cannot do that," he said. "It is most kind of you people, but we must be on our way."

"Yes," chimed in Father Ragueneau, "We are anxious to get back to Quebec."

But one of the men of Montreal smiled as he answered, "You have no choice, gentlemen. You see, the river beyond here is not yet open. There is no need to risk your lives further by chopping your route all the way to Quebec. "Be patient," he added, "We will take good care of you until the ice is gone."

"I am sure you will," Father Ragueneau replied.

And Monsieur du Puys shrugged his shoulders and smiled as he said, "I guess there is nothing else to do."

So the party lingered on in Montreal, waiting for the ice to break up. It was pleasant there, and Pierre and the others enjoyed their stay and the rest which they so sorely needed.

But they were glad when, two weeks later, news that the ice was breaking started them on their way once more.

As they waved farewell to their friends at Montreal, and headed out into the river, Pierre turned his eager thoughts toward Three Rivers and home. How good it would be to see his own people again! He had had enough of roaming — at least for some time. And, rested from their arduous trip, the other men seemed to share the same thought, for they all were paddling as vigorously as they could.

When, at last, the shore line began to grow familiar, Pierre's eagerness knew no bounds. Father Ragueneau steered his canoe over to Pierre's and smiled at him.

"You can hardly wait, can you, my son?"

"No, Father. I wish we could hurry."

Those in the canoe with Pierre redoubled their efforts, and shot ahead of the rest. But the others were not to be outdone, and, shouting back and forth to each other, they, too, increased their speed.

So it was that the happy and grateful group came within sight of the familiar fortress of Three Rivers. As they reached the shore, many excitedly waving and shouting inhabitants were already pouring outside the stockade gate to greet them.

As Father Ragueneau raised his eyes in time to return the greetings, he called across to Pierre.

"Pierre, my son, we are back just in time for the Easter Festival. It will be a double celebration for us all this year."

"Yes, Father," replied Pierre. But he could say no more, for, just then, he had caught sight of his mother and father and Margaret, and his throat had a sudden lump in it. As he jumped from the canoe and ran to meet his hurrying family, all he could think of was, "I am home again! Home! Thank God for that!"

REFERENCE MATERIAL CONSULTED

"RADISSON'S VOYAGES" — published by Prince Society, Boston

"STORY OF THE STATE OF NEW YORK" — Horne

"LA NAISANCE DES TROIS-RIVIERES" — Montarville Boucher de la Bruere

"NARRATIVE OF THE NEW NETHERLANDS" — ed. by J. Franklin Jameson

"HISTORY OF JEFFERSON AND ST. LAWRENCE COUNTIES" — Franklin Hough

"JESUIT RELATIONS" — Volume 36, 42, 43, 44

"COLONIAL DAYS IN NEW ENGLAND" —

"OUR INDIANS" — Verrill

"ALBANY, DUTCH, ENGLISH, AND AMERICAN" — Codman Hislop

"THE LONG HOUSE OF THE IROQUOIS" — Spencer L. Adams

"ALBANY CHRONICLES" — Cuyler Reynolds

"DUTCH NEW YORK" — Esther Singleton

"KING OF THE FUR TRADERS" — Vestal

"HISTORY OF NEW FRANCE" — Charlevoix

Reference books: "ENCYCLOPEDIA BRITANNICA" and the "WORLD BOOK"